How to KEEP
Your HARD-EARNED
MONEY

THE TAX SAVING
HANDBOOK FOR THE
SELF-EMPLOYED

HENRY AIY'M FELLMAN

Published by Solutions Press, Inc. ™
Boulder, Colorado

Copyright © 1996 by Henry Aiy'm Fellman

> **"This publication is designed to provide accurate and authoritative information in regard to the subject matter covered. It is sold with the understanding that the publisher is not engaged in rendering legal, accounting, or other professional service. If legal advice or other expert assistance is required, the services of a competent professional person should be sought."**

From a declaration of principles jointly adopted by a committee of the American Bar Association and a committee of publishers.

Library of Congress Cataloging-in-Publication Data

Fellman, Henry Aiy'm.
   How to keep your hard-earned money : the tax-saving handbook for the self-employed / by Henry Aiy'm Fellman
   p. cm.
   Includes index.
   Preassigned LCCN: 95-71209.
   ISBN 0-9648715-05-5
   1. Small business--Taxation--Law and legislation--United States. 2. Tax planning--United States. I. Title.
KF6491.F45 1996   343.73'068
                      QBI95-20484

DEDICATION

This book is written for all the hard working Americans who have set out on their own, in the good ol' American entrepreneur spirit, and are trying to make ends meet—not earning so much money that they can take advantage of the tax loopholes afforded the rich, yet earning too much to avoid paying taxes. This book is for the people who bear the brunt of the tax burden.

ACKNOWLEDGEMENTS

From the time I sat down to write this book it was less than six months for it to be ready for the printer. However, it also took years of preparation. Starting college as an accounting major in 1968 and finishing law school in 1975 accounted for my years of academic training. But, the information contained in this book is the product of over twenty years of finding ways to help clients lower their taxes, and learning what most people are willing and able to do. I owe my clients much gratitude for giving me the opportunity to learn my profession.

After writing the first draft I felt great! I had finished my first book. Little did I know that was the easy part. The next step was to put it into readable English and design the pages to be more reader friendly. The thanks for that go to my editor and graphics designer, John Passaro, who did a wonderful job in making this book into what it is.

It is more exceptional than usual for someone to conceive an idea and then meet no obstacles on the road to its fruition. My experience writing this book was no exception. Thanks to the persistent encouragement and injections of confidence by Donna and my parents I was able to stay on course and reach my goal.

I also wish to express many thanks to Jim Marty, CPA, President of Jim Marty and Company, as well as Kathy Leonard, President, Center for Responsible Investing, for their expertise and guidance regarding the maze of laws, rules and regulations that is the tax code.

And, it has been a pleasure once again teaming up with Johann Robbins. Because of his unique skills and talents the information presented in this book will be able to reach and help more people than I would have otherwise imagined possible.

TABLE OF CONTENTS

PREFACE

ROSCOE EGGER, JR., FORMER commissioner of the IRS has stated, "Any tax practitioner, any tax administrator, any taxpayer who has worked with the Internal Revenue Code knows that it is probably the biggest mishmash of statutes imaginable."

It is so complex that Albert Einstein was prompted to say, "The hardest thing in the world to understand is income tax." If it's that difficult to understand even for one of the smartest people who ever lived, how is the average taxpayer supposed to put it to use?

As Ronald Reagan is reported to have said, "The government has the nerve to tell the people of the country, 'You figure out how much you owe us, and we can't help you because our people don't understand it either; and if you make a mistake, we'll make you pay a penalty for making the mistake.'"

It's no wonder most taxpayers—those who can't afford to pay the exorbitant rates charged by most lawyers and CPAs—end up paying far more taxes than the law requires.

Early in my career, my work at a Big 8 CPA firm included saving lots of money for the very rich. However, after a while I realized that helping them afford a second yacht or fly to Paris for lunch was not fulfilling to me—which is why I've spent the last 17 years working with small businesses. I've found it a much more rewarding and satisfying experience helping people make enough money to put food on their table, a roof over their heads, and enjoy life.

Three years ago, I began visiting my clients in their homes to prepare their tax returns, instead of meeting in my office. This has been a wonderful experience. When I go to my clients' homes—babies crying, children playing, the buzz of activity throughout the house—I get more of a feel for their lives. And, they get to experience me as more than a stuffed shirt with a noose around my neck.

Recently, I expanded these activities by creating affordable, quality workshops and publications to help self-employed people make their small business more profitable. This book is a part of that effort.

In this book, I show self-employed individuals how to take advantage of the tax code and get BIG Tax Saving Deductions.

All the tax saving techniques presented are 100 percent legal. Not only are these techniques absolutely legal, but I've presented them in plain, everyday English with easy-to-follow, step-by-step instructions.

HOW TO PUT THIS BOOK TO GOOD USE

JOHN, A SELF-EMPLOYED artist and a friend of mine, read an early draft of this book and told me, "This book is just what I need. I could really use a lot of the tax saving strategies presented in this book. But I'm afraid I won't be able to do what's required to put the ideas to use." That bothered me. If the readers didn't use the Tax Saving Strategies presented in this book, the whole purpose of the book would be defeated. So I added features to make the book even more user friendly, including a very practical and easy-to-use method to put the Tax Saving Strategies into action.

I wrote this book because I wanted to help self-employed individuals save on the amount of taxes they pay without having to pay the exorbitant fees of accountants and lawyers. The Tax Saving Strategies are presented in easy-to-understand, everyday English, and with east-to-follow, step-by-step instructions. So I became concerned when John told me that he still wasn't sure he would ever really apply the information to his business, even though he knew that by doing so he could save thousands of dollars every year.

I want you to read and understand the information in this book. But, even more importantly, I want you to put these tax saving ideas into use. To help you implement these Tax Saving Strategies, I've included a feature to help you set up a non-threatening program of implementation. This program is designed to help you identify which tax saving strategies will help you most and which are easiest for you to put into effect. And, then to implement them one at a time instead of getting overwhelmed trying to do them all at once—with the result that you put it all on the back burner and never get to it.

At the end of each chapter there is a scorecard. This scorecard will be used to rate each Tax Saving Strategy presented in that chapter as to its ease of implementation and its potential Tax Saving Benefit.

The following is the schedule for rating:

Ease of Implementation:

    3 - easy
    2 - average
    1 - difficult

Tax Saving Benefit:

    3 - save lots of money
    2 - save a medium amount of money
    1 - save only a little amount of money

The last chapter will explain how to put the scorecards of each chapter together and develop a step-by-step strategy of implementation.

Chapter 1

AUDIT MYTHS AND OTHER TALES OF HORROR

A.K.A.
GIVE UNTO CAESAR WHAT IS CAESAR'S
... BUT NOT A PENNY MORE

Many law-abiding, upstanding citizens refuse to take all the tax saving deductions we are perfectly entitled to.

T HAT'S BECAUSE WE'RE petrified of being audited by the IRS. We've been led to believe that if we take certain deductions, like the home-office deduction, we're in effect begging the IRS to audit us. Just by claiming certain perfectly legitimate deductions, we'll red flag our return for an audit.

IRS audits are one of the biggest fears in this country. People come to me literally shaking because they received a NOTICE from the IRS. In fact, it's not unusual for a client to call me up almost in tears because they received a letter from the IRS. They ask, "What will I do?" I ask what the letter says, and they tell me, "I don't know. I haven't opened it yet."

One woman refused to open an IRS letter until she was in my presence. Then she made me open it. It turned out she had filled her tax return out improperly and overstated her income. The IRS was informing her she was getting an additional refund!

The first time I represented a client at an IRS audit, I was as scared as my client. I had no idea what to expect. But when it was over, my client ended up with a refund. Boy, was I relieved.

This is not to say that you don't have reason to fear the IRS. There are many stories of ruthless and abusive IRS agents. And, many of those stories are probably true. However, extreme tactics are usually saved for suspected criminals, tax evaders, and politics. I've been representing taxpayers for over 15 years and I personally know of only two incidents where the IRS used excessive force or ruthless tactics. One case involved a suspected drug dealer who hadn't filed a tax return for ten years, and the other was probably politically motivated.

That's not to say that it's okay for the IRS to ever act that way. But, the point is if you're the average taxpayer, you don't have to worry that you'll be treated that way.

What most people don't realize is that the IRS wants you to be scared of being audited. They want you to think that they're like the KGB. They want you to be too terrified to cheat on your tax return. That's why they go after celebrities and prominent taxpayers who are more likely to make a splash on the front pages.

And, in a lot of these cases, they'll intentionally give them a hard time so that you won't even think of trying to cheat the government (or, at least not as much as you would have otherwise.)

It's also important to keep in mind that the IRS is a business. Part of their business is collecting taxes and making sure taxpayers pay at least what the law requires them to pay. The IRS, however, doesn't have the necessary number of agents to check over two-hundred million

In 1992, less than one percent (less than one in one hundred) tax returns filed by Schedule C filers were audited.

(that's 200,000,000) tax returns filed every year. They can't possibly stay on top of every return. What's their solution? They audit taxpayers who potentially will yield the most tax revenues. That's why the chance of getting audited is so slim. In 1992, less than one percent of tax returns filed by Schedule C filers were audited.

Senator Henry Bellmon was quoted in 1969 as saying, "In a recent conversation with an official at the Internal Revenue Service, I was amazed when he told me that, 'If the taxpayers of this country ever discover that the IRS operates on 90 percent bluff, the entire system will collapse.'"

I am not recommending that you cheat on your tax returns.

I strongly recommend that you pay your taxes as required by law.

What you'd save by filing a falsified tax return is not worth the restlessness, loss of sleep, and worry you'll suffer over the next three or, in some cases, seven years.

So—pay your taxes, but take the deductions that are due you! If you don't, you're doing yourself, your family, and this country a terrible disservice. It is your RIGHT to take all the deductions allowed by law. It's an aberration of our legal system for the IRS to perpetrate fear in citizens of this country to do what is their right to do.

As the Supreme Court Justice Learned Hand said, "... nobody owes any public duty to pay more than the law demands: taxes are enforced exactions, not voluntary contributions. To demand more in the name of morals is mere cant."

Guilty Until Proven Innocent

T HE BASIC TENET OF THE American legal system is that one is presumed innocent until proven guilty. That means if you are suspected of breaking the law the government must show proof of your guilt.

You are presumed innocent and don't have to offer proof as to your innocence. This doctrine, incorporated into The Bill of Rights by our country's forefathers, was considered essential to guarantee freedom to its citizens.

This basic tenet of innocence has been sanctified in every area of our legal system—except one: Tax Law. Under the tax law, you are effectively presumed guilty until proven innocent. This book is not intended to be a political dissertation on the IRS, so I will not discuss the legitimacy of this deviation from our Bill of Rights. But, it is important for you to realize that's what you're dealing with if you get audited.

Throughout this book I will be emphasizing a basic principle.

For every deduction you claim, you must be able to

SUBSTANTIATE!

SUBSTANTIATE!

SUBSTANTIATE!

If you can't substantiate a deduction, you'll be presumed to be, in effect, lying and the deduction will be disallowed. The IRS is not required to prove the deduction isn't valid. It's your burden of proof to prove it is valid. And, it's the same with income. For every deposit indicated on your bank statement, you must prove it isn't income or it will be presumed to be income and subject to tax. For example, if you get a gift of $500 from your family on your birthday and you deposit it in your bank, you must offer proof, if asked, that the $500 was other than taxable earned income.

In the following chapters, every time I alert you to what you need to do in order to fulfill the substantiation requirements of the IRS please take it seriously—very seriously. If you follow my simple instructions, in the highly unlikely event you do get audited, you will feel assured your deductions will be allowed.

The Tax System and the Self-Employed: A Basic Overview

T HROUGHOUT THIS BOOK I will give you hypothetical examples showing the Tax Saving Benefit you can receive by the various strategies offered. To help you understand the basis of these benefits, I'm going to give you a basic overview of the tax system as it applies to self-employed individuals.

As a self-employed individual, the profit from your business is actually subject to three taxes—federal income tax, state income tax (unless your state doesn't have one), and self-employment tax.

The federal income tax is a graduated tax. That is, as your income gets higher, the tax rate increases. However, when you go into a higher tax bracket, you don't pay the higher rate on all your income—just on the amount over the lower tax bracket. For example, if in 1994 you filed as married filing jointly, the first $38,000 of your taxable income was taxed at 15 percent. The next $53,850 was taxed at 28 percent. The next $48,150 was taxed at 31 percent, and so on.

So, if you're married filing a joint return and your taxable income is $40,000, the tax on the first $38,000 will be $5,700 (15 percent of $38,000). The next $2,000 will be taxed at the 28 percent rate for $560, for a total tax of $6260. Refer to the Tax Rate Schedule in Appendix A, which shows the tax brackets for each different filing status.

Each state and city sets up their own income tax structure. I couldn't possibly list each state's and each city's income tax rates here in this book. Throughout this book, we are assuming that the state tax is five percent of taxable income, and that there is no city income tax.

Throughout this book, we are assuming that the state tax is five percent of taxable income, and that there is no city income tax.

The self-employment tax is the self-employed individual's version of the FICA or social security tax. As you probably know, employers and employees are responsible for paying a percentage of the employee's earnings into the social security system and Medicare. (As of 1994, the amount paid by each is 7.65 percent of the first $57,600. The small Medicare percentage continues for wages in excess of $57,600.)

For FICA purposes, self-employed individuals are not considered employees—instead of the FICA tax, they pay a self-employment tax. The rate is the same as the employer's and employee's rate combined— 15.3 percent. And, it has the same ceiling limits as

FICA. When you pay the self-employment tax, you are entitled to a deduction for one-half the tax. In effect, the rate for the self-employment tax is approximately 13 percent of the first $57,600 (for 1994) of your profit.

For each example presented in this book the tax savings will be based on the following assumptions:

➤ The taxpayer is filing a joint return

➤ The federal income tax bracket is 28 percent

➤ The taxpayer is subject to a state income tax rate of five percent, and

➤ The effective self-employment tax is 13 percent

➤ The amount subject to self-employment tax is less than $57,600

Note: Your profit plus your wage earnings that do not exceed the ceiling ($57,600 for 1994) will not be subject to the self-employment tax.

Profit from business	$_____
PLUS: Wage earnings	$_____
SUB-TOTAL	$_____
LESS: Ceiling $57,600 for 1994	$_____
AMOUNT NOT SUBJECT	
TO SELF-EMPLOYMENT TAX:	$_____

Now, let's move on to the nitty-gritty!

Chapter 2

IF YOU'RE ENTITLED TO THE HOME-OFFICE DEDUCTION— TAKE IT!

It's tax time. Inevitably, some clients come to me and say, "I operate my business out of my home but I don't want to take a home-office deduction."

THEY'VE HEARD THAT if they take that deduction it would be like waving a red flag in the face of the IRS begging to be audited. As Pat Paulsen used to say on the old Smothers Brothers Show—"POPPYCOCK!"

I say, if you're entitled to a home-office deduction then by all means take it! Unless, you decide you want to make a donation to the IRS. In fact, I'd rather you make a donation—at least you'd get a deduction for a charitable contribution.

The fact is, in 17 years I have yet to experience or hear of anyone getting audited just because they took a home-office deduction.

Tax Saving Benefits for Operating Your Business Out of Your Home

W HETHER YOU OWN or rent, if you work out of your home, a portion of its costs might entitle you to significant Tax Savings Deductions. If your home office qualifies, you may deduct the business portion of the cost of owning or renting your house, including depreciation, home mortgage interest, rent, utilities, repairs, and maintenance. This can amount to a sizable Tax Saving Deduction.

Let's say you own your home and use 15 percent of it for business. You rent the house at $1500 per month, your utilities cost $120 each month, and the repairs and maintenance cost you $1,000 for the year. That's a total out of pocket expense of $20,440 for the year. Of that amount, 15 percent is a business expense, which gives you a $3,066 business deduction. Assuming a federal tax bracket of 28 percent and a state tax bracket of 5 percent and an effective self-employment tax of 13 percent, the net tax savings will be $1410. That's an extra $1410 in your pocket. Do you really want to throw that money away?

CALCULATE YOUR TAX SAVINGS

1. **Percent of home used for business** _____

2. **Expenses allowed as Itemized Deduction or Business Deduction:**

   a. Home Mortgage Interest $_____

   b. Real Estate Taxes $_____

   c. Total $_____

3. **Line 1 X Line 2c** $_____

4. **Tax Saving #1**

   [Line 3 X .13 (self-employment tax)] $_____

5. **Other home deductions:**

   a. Rent or Depreciation $_____

   b. Utilities $_____

   c. House Insurance $_____

   d. Repairs and Maintenance $_____

   e. Miscellaneous $_____

   f. Total other home deductions $_____

6. **Line 1 X Line 5f** $_____

7. **Your Tax Rate:**

   a. Federal Income Tax Rate   ._____

   b. State Income Tax Rate   ._____

c. Self-Employment Tax Rate	. 13_____
(Adjust if not all earnings are subject to self-employment tax. Please see note on page 22.)	
d. Total Tax Rate	._____
8. Tax Savings #2 (Line 6 X Line 7d)	$_____
9. YOUR TAX SAVINGS (Line 4 + Line 8)	$_____

Your automobile is another major, though often overlooked, Tax Saving Deduction benefit of operating your office out of your home. This subject is discussed in detail in Chapter 3, Getting the Most "TSPM" Out of Your Car.

Does Your Office at Home Qualify?

I F YOU RENT AN OFFICE outside your home, there's no question the cost is tax deductible. And, what's more, the IRS wouldn't care if you use the space for activities unrelated to your business. You could watch TV there, play chess, take naps, play computer games. It wouldn't matter. The cost of the space would still be deductible.

But, if you move that same office and everything in it to your home, all of a sudden the deduction comes into question. If you do anything in that space that's not related to your business, or it you don't meet certain other requirements, the cost of that space is no longer deductible.

Fair? NO! But what do you expect? It's the Tax Code.

There are a few situations where taxpayers are entitled to a home-office deduction without having to be concerned with meeting many of the major requirements. If you run a day-care operation out of your home on a regular, continuing basis, the portion of your home used for the business is deductible. No problem. If you store inventory at your home on a regular, continuing basis and your home is the only fixed location for your business, the space used to store inventory is deductible. No problem. If your home-office is in a separate structure not attached to your residence, such as a studio, detached garage, or barn, then it's deductible. No problem as long as the space is used on a regular, continuing basis and exclusively for your business.

Most taxpayers who work out of their homes do not fit in one of those categories. For their home-office to qualify as a deduction, it must pass one of two tests. To pass the first test you must meet ALL the following requirements.

1. The portion of your home used for business must be used EXCLUSIVELY for your trade or business. And, EXCLUSIVELY means EXCLUSIVELY! It cannot be used for any other purpose. Your kids can't play computer games in that space, you can't watch the Super Bowl there, you can't make your personal calls from the phone in the office.

2. The space must be used on a regular, continuous basis.

3. And, your home must be used to meet with patients, clients, or customers. However, this doesn't mean you can meet with one of your clients once or twice a

year and qualify. It's not that easy. You must meet
with them at your home-office on a regular basis,
during the normal course of the day and it must be
substantial and integral to the conduct of your business.

If you don't meet all the requirements of the first
test, you aren't out of the game yet. You can still take
a deduction for the use of your home if you meet ALL
the requirements of the second test.

1. As in the first test, the portion of your home used for
   business must be used EXCLUSIVELY for your trade
   or business.

2. The space must be used on a regular, continuous
   basis.

3. And, your home must be your "principal place of
   business."

How do you determine whether your home-office is
your "principle place of business?" The law says that
you look at all the facts and circumstances to determine if it is or is not.

Obviously if your home-office is the only fixed location of your business and is the place where you
perform all services then it's your principle place of
business. An example of this would be a writer who
does all their writing from their home and promotes
their material via phone and mail. However, for most
businesses it isn't that clear cut.

In a landmark decision, known as the Soliman
Case, the U.S. Supreme Court helped clarify how to
determine the principle place of business. Unfortunately, the decision went against the taxpayer, Dr.

Soliman, and left many business owners and tax professionals with the impression that the home-office deduction was virtually wiped out. But that's utter nonsense!

First of all, if you passed one of the other tests, you're entitled to the home-office deduction regardless of whether it's your primary place of business. If not, it's still possible you can satisfy the principle place of business requirement.

In order to determine whether your home-office is considered your "primary place of business," it's necessary to consider the following two primary factors:

First factor: Look at the relative importance of the business activities performed at each location you do business. Where do the activities that are most important to your business take place? Where do your income-generating tasks take place? And, most important, where do you meet with clients or deliver your goods or services?

If, after considering those questions, you are still unable to determine your principle place of business, consider the following:

Second factor: Analyze the time spent at each location where you do business. Usually the place you spend more than 50 percent of your time is your principle place of business. If you still can't determine your principle place of business, it's possible you don't have one, and your home will not qualify as your principle place of business.

Here's some examples to help you understand all these rules and how they might apply to your situation.

Situation #1: Let's say you're a self-employed plumber. You repair and install plumbing in your customers' homes. Generally, you spend 40 hours each week in the field and ten hours each week at your home-office doing paper work, working with blue prints, and talking to your customers on the phone. If you were the plumber, would you take a deduction for an office at home? If you did and the IRS audited you, they would probably disallow the deduction. That's because the place where the plumber did the work that earned him his or her money was not at home. Even if he employed a full-time secretary who worked for him exclusively in the home-office, he still couldn't take the deduction.

Situation #2: Let's say you teach at a local college. You spend 25 hours in the classroom and 35 hours at your home-office doing work related to what you teach. Your work at home might be essential, but your most important work will be deemed to take place at school and therefore you will not be entitled to a home-office deduction.

Situation #3: Let's say you're a writer who spends 35 hours each week writing at your home-office. You spend, on average, another 15 hours each week doing research and meeting with publishers and interviewees. Are you going to be able to safely take a home-office deduction? You bet!

Situation #4: Let's say you sell costume jewelry at craft shows, to retail stores, and through the mail. You spend 25 hours each week at home processing orders, keeping books, and ordering supplies. You also spend 15 hours each week at craft shows and at retail stores. Each of the activities generate approximately the same amount of money. Would you take a home-office deduction if you were in this situation? You bet! Since there is no significant income difference as to where you earn your money, you look at the time spent at each location. You spend the most time at home. Therefore, you are entitled to the home-office deduction.

Here's some things you might be able to do to turn your home-office into a Tax Saving Deduction. You know your situation best. With a little creativity, most businesses can be set up to qualify for this deduction.

➤ IF POSSIBLE, MEET WITH your clients at your house *and* keep records of the meetings. Do you remember the good ol' days when doctors made house calls? Well, today, if house calls account for most of their patients, they lose their home-office deduction.

➤ IF YOU HAVE MORE THAN one work location, try to work at least 50 percent of the time at home *and* document your hours.

➤ IN GENERAL, TRY TO SPEND more time working at home and try to arrange it so you do the more important tasks at your home office.

➤ IF YOU SELL PRODUCTS, have your customers pick up the goods at your home.

➤ IF YOU MEET WITH PATIENTS or do consulting work, don't meet your clients or patients at their home or office, have them come to you. In addition to giving you a Tax Saving Deduction for the business use of your home, it will save you something else that we're all short of—TIME.

➤ USE A STRUCTURE THAT is not attached to your house.

Exclusive Means 100-Percent Exclusive

T HROUGHOUT THIS CHAPTER I make it clear that in most cases the space used for your office must be used EXCLUSIVELY for your business. That means that space cannot be used for *any* personal use during the tax year.

That means you can't watch TV there, your kids can't do homework on the computer, and you can't use the phone for personal calls.

In fact, if you operate more than one business out of your office at home, both of them must qualify for the home-office deduction or neither of them will.

This also applies in the situation where you have a second job outside your home. If you take work home

31

from that job and do that work in your home-office then you could be disqualified from taking the home-office deduction for even the business that qualifies for it.

✍️ **TIP** Remove all non-business related items from the space used as your office.

✍️ **TIP** Although the office portion of your home must be used exclusively for business, it does not need to be a separate room. It can be any space that's just used for your business. And, even though it does not need to be partitioned, it helps if you have some way to establish the line of demarcation. For example, you can use a bookcase as the dividing line.

Avoiding IRS Hassles

THE KEY IS AS FOLLOWS:

Document!

Document!

Document!

➤ KEEP A RECORD OF your times in and out of the office.

➤ KEEP LOGS SHOWING who you met with, where, when, and why.

➤ KEEP RECORDS OF the nature of the work you perform at home and elsewhere so you can substantiate that the most important tasks related to your work took place at home. This is important if you work out of your home and also perform services elsewhere.

➤ HAVE PROOF THAT YOU used a portion of your home for your business.

➤ TAKE PICTURES. TAKE LOTS of pictures that will help you prove the location in the house and the size of the room. Take pictures of business equipment and desks in the room and make sure that nothing of a personal nature (like a bed) was in the room. You can even throw in a newspaper to help prove the date the pictures were taken.

Determining the Percentage of Your Home Used for Your Business

O BVIOUSLY, THE MORE of your home you are able to claim for business, the greater your home-office deduction will be. The IRS allows two methods for determining the percentage of your home used for business.

The first method is dividing the square footage of the area used for business by the total square footage of your home.

If all the rooms in your home are approximately the same size, you are allowed to use the second method: divide the number of rooms used for business by the total number of rooms in your home. This is quicker—it may end up a higher or lower percentage.

Watch Out for the Pitfall!

HERE'S A PITFALL TO the home-office deduction that many people fall into. Once you know it, you will not be prey to it because you will know how to avoid falling into the trap.

Normally if you own your home and sell it for a profit, you aren't required to pay tax on the gain as long as you reinvest the proceeds in another home within two years of the sale.

However, here's the pitfall: if you were entitled to a home-office deduction, the portion of the gain attributed to the part of your house you deducted is subject to income tax.

Here's a pitfall: if you were entitled to a home-office deduction, the portion of the gain attributed to that part of your house is subject to income tax.

For instance, if 15 percent of your home qualifies for the home-office deduction, 15 percent of the gain on the sale of your home will be included in your taxable income. That's a nasty ending to a great deduction. Here's how to get around it. In the year of the sale, make sure your office disqualifies for the home-office deduction.

It's easy. Remember, in order to qualify for the home-office deduction the space must be used exclusively for business. That is, you can't do anything in there during the year that's not related to your business. Therefore, at any time during the year, take pictures which show the room was used for an activity that disqualifies it as a home-office. For example, put the TV in there and throw a Super Bowl party, or let the kids play on the computer. (Whatever you do, make it fun. After all, you're saving money.)

Another pitfall with regards to the sale of a residence that's been used for a home-office is the possible loss of the once-in-a-lifetime exclusion from the gain on the sale of a residence. If you're 55 years old or older and realize a gain on the sale of your residence, you're entitled to exclude the first $125,000 of that gain. This is a once-in-a-lifetime exclusion. Once you use the exclusion, even if it's for less than the full $125,000, that's it—you don't get to take it again. As in the first pitfall I described above, if a portion of the home sold is used as a home-office, that portion does not qualify for the exclusion. The rule is not based on just the previous year, but on any two of the past five years; that is, if the part used for business does not qualify for the home-office deduction for at least any two of the last five years, you are okay and don't lose any part of the exclusion. Also, if you discontinue business use of your residence in the year of sale, you won't lose the exclusion.

By the way, you don't have to worry about this if the non-business portion of your gain would be $125,000 or more. Once you hit that amount, you can't take any more anyway, so the business portion wouldn't add to your savings.

TIP What if you sell your house at a loss? If part of the house qualified for the home-office deduction, be sure to maintain that status until the date of sale. That's because the portion of the loss attributed to your office will be deductible.

☞ TAX SAVING ACTION STEPS YOU CAN TAKE TODAY

CREATING A HOME-OFFICE DEDUCTION

☑ Set aside a portion of your house for your business use. It could be a room or even just a portion of a room.

☑ Remove all personal, non-business related belongings.

☑ Take pictures of the room. To help prove the date you can include a picture of a newspaper with that day's headlines. However, unless you are a sports reporter, don't show the sports section.

☑ Use that space exclusively for business.

☑ Meet there with patients, clients or customers on a regular basis. Or, make sure it qualifies as your principal place of business.

☑ Keep a brief log of how much time you work at home and at other regular business locations (if you have any), and record what you do there.

Scorecard

Tax Saving Strategy	Ease of Implementation	Tax Saving Benefits
	3 - easy to implement 2 - average to implement 1 - difficult to implement	3 - save lots of $ 2 - save some $ 1 - save little $
Set up a deductible office at your home		

Chapter 3

GETTING THE MOST "TSPM" OUT OF YOUR CAR

Using your automobile can give you big TSPM (Tax Savings Per Mile). However, many people either overlook it entirely or don't take full advantage of it because of the misconception that the required record keeping is too cumbersome.

T HAT WAS TRUE ONCE upon a time but, fortunately, those same record keeping requirements also applied to our lawmakers. They didn't like doing it either, so they changed the law to make it simpler.

Once upon a time, to deduct the use of your automobile, you were required to keep contemporaneous records of the date, location, purpose, and mileage of the trip. We had to log our beginning and ending odometer readings of each trip. Isn't that absurd? Like most everyone else, I had a difficult time remembering to jot down the information. I even tried keeping a string that was attached to my log dangling in front of my face at the driver's seat. But that didn't always work either.

Most people I knew never even attempted a log. They either didn't bother with the deduction or lied. As Will Rogers once said, "The Income Tax has made more liars out of the American people than golf has."

As Will Rogers once said, "The Income Tax has made more liars out of the American people than golf has."

How much is the deduction for the use of your car worth?

Let's say you drive on the average 20 miles each day for your business. That's about 5,000 miles for the year, which translates into a minimum deduction Tax Saving Deduction of $1,450 ($0.29 each mile). Assuming an effective tax rate of 46 percent (income and self-employment taxes) your tax savings for the use of your automobile is $666. Would you even consider going down to your local IRS office and handing them a check for $666, saying, "Keep up the good work?" That's in effect what you are doing by not taking this deduction.

CALCULATE YOUR TAX SAVINGS

1. Total Business Miles Driven This Year   _____

2. Standard Rate Per Mile ($0.29 for 1994) X   . _____

3. Standard Mileage Deduction   _____

4. Federal Income Tax Rate   . _____

5. State Income Tax Rate   . _____

6. Self-Employment Tax Rate   .13 _____

(Adjust if not all earnings are subject to self-employment tax. Please see note on page 22.)

7. Total Tax Rate X (lines 4+5+16)   _____

8. YOUR TAX SAVINGS (line 3 x line 7)   _____

THE EZ MILEAGE LOG

U NDER THE CURRENT LAW it is no longer a big deal to maintain the necessary log and records. All you need to record is the number of business miles and total miles (business and non-business) driven during the year. You must substantiate the date, where you went, and the business purpose.

There are two methods you can use for computing this deduction. One is the actual method and the other is the standard rate method. They will be discussed in detail later. If you compute this deduction using the actual method then you will also need to substantiate the cost of gas, repairs, maintenance, insurance, and registration.

Here's all you have to do. At the beginning of each year jot down on January 1st the number of miles your odometer shows. During the year, next to the name of any appointments you have, record the number of miles and circle that number. Also, jot down other business related stops, such as the bank, office supply store, and post office. For most of your stops, the business purpose will be obvious. If not, jot down a short explanation.

At the end of the year (or first day of the new year) record your odometer reading again. Then, all you do is subtract the odometer reading at the beginning of the year from the end of the year—that gives you the total miles you drove for the year. Then, add up all the circled numbers, and that gives you the business miles for the year.

If you use the actual method, keep all your car-related receipts in one envelope or folder and add them up at the end of the year. An even easier way to do it is make sure you pay for all car-related expenses with a credit card, then you just pull them off your monthly statements. Some of my clients even take it one step further and dedicate one of their credit cards exclusively to car-related expenses.

Converting Non-Deductible Commuting Expenses into a Tax Saving Deduction

T HE TAX LAW ALLOWS US to deduct any and all ordinary and necessary expenses incurred in a trade or business for the production of income. So shouldn't the cost of going to and from your home and work be deductible? Isn't it necessary for you to make the trip to earn money? Sure it is. For many people commuting is not only very time consuming but puts a lot of miles on your vehicle. But the IRS has made a unique transportation category called "commuting expenses," and has declared that those expenses are not deductible.

Commuting expenses include all transportation expenses, (such as mileage, tolls, bus, and taxi) to and from your residence and your *regular* place of business.

By the way, some of you might be thinking, "I know how to get around this. I'll use commuting time to make business calls on my cellular phone." Or, "I can drive with my partner to work and discuss business." You are not the first to come up with those ideas. Unfortunately, they have not worked.

But, here's what you can do.

Situation #1: If you have a *regular* place of business, all transportation expenses to *temporary* work locations are deductible. That means if you have a regular business location, whether at home or elsewhere, and you go directly from your home to a customer or to your bank or your office supply store, those transportation expenses will be deductible. So, if on the way to your office you stop at the post office and on the way home you stop to see a client, all your travels for the day will be deductible.

WATCH OUT!

If you stop at a particular client too often, the IRS will consider the site as one of your regular places of business and will not allow the deduction. The moral is, keep arranging your travels at the beginning and end of your work day so that you are not always going to the same place.

It is possible that you don't have a *regular* place of business. In that case, none of your transportation costs, even to temporary work sites, will be deductible. However, if the temporary location is outside the metropolitan area you ordinarily work in, then transportation costs to that location will be deductible.

Situation #2: Remember our discussion on the home-office deduction in the previous chapter? Well, here's another benefit of having your office at home. If you qualify for a home-office deduction, all transportation expenses to and from your home, for any business-related purpose, are deductible. And that rule applies even for traveling to another regular place of business.

PUT ON YOUR THINKING CAPS: What if your home is a regular place of business but it doesn't qualify for a home-office deduction?

Are your transportation expenses between your home and another regular place of business deductible? For example, remember our plumber friend in the last chapter whose office at home didn't qualify for the home-office deduction? Here's a surprise. The courts have ruled that even though he's not allowed a deduction for the use of his home, he can still deduct the costs of all transportation, such as the traveling costs to all his plumbing jobs around town.

Strange as it may seem, the IRS does not agree with this decision, and has announced that they will continue to challenge these deductions made by taxpayers.

Who should you listen to? If I were you, I would listen to the courts.

Actual Versus Standard—Which Do I Choose?

T HE STANDARD RATE METHOD is simple to compute. Just add up all your business miles and multiply that by the standard rate. In 1994, the standard rate was $0.29 (twenty-nine cents) per mile. Under the actual method, you need to add up all your automobile-related expenses, including depreciation, repairs, maintenance, tires, gas, oil, insurance, and registration fees, then multiply that by the percentage the car was used for business (business miles divided by total miles). Whichever method you choose you will also be able to deduct the business portion of parking fees, tolls, interest, and ownership tax.

Which should you choose? Obviously, the one which allows you the greater deduction. In general, if you have an inexpensive car ($4,000 or less) it's probably better to choose the standard mileage deduction because its depreciation will be low. However, since there are so many factors that can affect your decision, it's best to calculate the deduction both ways. Then choose the method that gives you the greater deduction. You can switch methods from year to year, but not if you choose the actual method and use accelerated depreciation instead of straight line depreciation.

The standard rate method is not available if your vehicle is for hire, such as a taxi,

OR if you lease your vehicle,

OR if you use two or more cars simultaneously for business.

☞ TAX SAVING ACTION STEPS YOU CAN TAKE TODAY

START A MILEAGE LOG

☑ In your appointment book, under today's date, record your odometer reading. If you can determine the odometer mileage as of a date closer to the beginning of the year that would be better.

HINT: *Look on repair invoices. Most auto mechanics record odometer readings on your bill.*

☑ Under today's date, list all the places you went for your business and next to each record the mileage and circle it. (If necessary, also record the purpose).

☑ Put all receipts for car-related expenses in a folder marked CAR RECEIPTS.

Scorecard

Tax Saving Strategy	Ease of Implementation	Tax Saving Benefits
	3 - easy to implement 2 - average to implement 1 - difficult to implement	3 - save lots of $ 2 - save some $ 1 - save little $
Keep a mileage log and record your car related expenses		
Convert commuting non-deductible expenses into a Tax Saving Deduction		

Chapter 4

WHEN IT PAYS TO HIRE YOUR FAMILY

Are you married? Do you have any children? Do you plan to get married? Do you plan to have children? If you answer Yes to any of these questions, this chapter is for you!

YOU CAN EARN LOTS OF TAX Saving Benefits by hiring your spouse and or children. In this chapter, you will learn the fundamentals of income splitting, how hiring your child reduces your self-employment tax, how your business can pay for and deduct the cost of your medical care and health insurance, and lots more tax saving tips earned by hiring family members. Also, at the end of the chapter, are instructions on what you have to do to stay audit safe.

Instead of Giving Your Children an Allowance, Pay Them a Salary

When you give an allowance to your child, is it deductible? No. When you buy clothes for your child, is that deductible? No. When you pay for your child's athletic equipment, is that deductible? No. When you put away money for your child's education, is that deductible? No.

But what if your child works for you in some capacity? Are their wages deductible? Sure they are! What if you include in their wage their allowance? It's still deductible. What if they pay for their share of the rent, their candy, their sporting goods, and put away money for college? The wages you pay them are still deductible. I'll bet you're starting to catch on.

What if your child works for you in some capacity? Are their wages deductible? Sure they are!

Let's do a little review of the tax system.

First: What kind of tax is the federal income tax? If you said graduated you are right. Remember, a graduated income tax means that the more money you make, a greater percentage of it goes to the IRS. For the 1994 tax year, there were five income tax brackets:

15 percent

28 percent

31 percent

36 percent

39.6 percent

For purposes of the illustration in this book we are assuming a 28-percent federal income tax bracket.

Second: Each state has it's own income tax laws. We're are assuming for the purposes of this book that the state income tax rate is five percent

Third: Do all self-employed people pay FICA? No. But, they pay a self-employment tax which is the equivalent to FICA.

Income Splitting

T HE GOAL OF INCOME SPLITTING is to shift your income that's taxed at a higher bracket into someone else's lower bracket. That is, if your taxable income is high enough to put you in the 28-percent bracket, you want to shift as much of that income that's being taxed at 28 percent into a lower tax bracket.

One way to do this is by shifting your taxable income to your children. If you are in the 28 percent bracket and your child's income is taxed at 15 percent, you will have effectively saved 13 percent of the amount you transferred.

Reducing the tax bracket is just the beginning of the benefits you can reap by hiring your child. Your child can also take advantage of the standard deduction, which in 1995 will be $3,900. This means the first $3,900 is not taxed at all! And, what's more, if they put $2,000 into their IRA, the first $5,900 will be tax free.

But wait, there's more! If your child is under 18 years old, the wages you pay them are not subject to FICA tax.

Now, let's put this all together. Let's say you hire your 16-year-old son to do janitorial and clerical work. He works part time during the school year and full time during the summer. The total wages you pay him amounts to $7,000 for the year. That means the wages paid him will be fully deductible by your business. Therefore, if you're like our hypothetical taxpayer, your tax savings will be reduced by $3,220 (46 percent of $7,000) As your child's tax will only be $220 (20 percent of $1,100), that's a whopping tax savings of $3,000!

Is there a minimum age required for your child to work for you? NO! Just, make sure they performed real work and are paid a reasonable wage. The tax court has allowed parents to deduct wages paid to their children as young as seven years old. But check with your state for child labor laws pertaining to minimum age requirements.

CALCULATE
YOUR TAX SAVINGS

1. Annual Wages Paid Your Child $_____

2. Your Federal Income Tax Rate   ._____

3. Your State Income Tax Rate   ._____

4. Your Self-Employment Tax Rate   .13_____

(Adjust if not all earnings are subject to self-employment tax. Please see note on page 22.)

5. Your Total Tax Rate (Lines 2+3+4)   ._____

6. Your Tax Saving (Line 5 x Line 1) $_____

7. Child's Standard Deduction
   ($3,900 for 1995) $_____

8. Child's IRA Contribution $_____

9. Child's Deduction (Line 7 + Line 8) $_____

10. Child's Taxable Income (Line 1-Line 9) $_____

11. Child's Federal Income Tax Rate   ._____

12. Child's State Income Tax Rate   ._____

13. Child's FICA Tax (zero if under 18)   ._____

14. Child's Total Tax Rate
    (Line 11+12+13)   ._____

15. Child's Tax (Line 1 x Line 14) $_____

16. YOUR TOTAL FAMILY TAX SAVINGS
    (Line 6 - Line 15) $_____

WARNING! Be sure you pay for more than 50 percent of your child's living expenses, or else you will lose your child as a tax dependent. You can have your cake and eat it too, if you know how to play by their rules and put them to your advantage.

Tax Benefits of Hiring Your Spouse—Health Insurance and Other Medical Expenses

I 'M SURE I DON'T HAVE to tell you about the high cost of health insurance. If you have coverage it's probably making a big dent in your budget. For some, the cost might be prohibitive. Wouldn't it be nice if the government helped make health insurance more affordable by footing some of the bill?

As you know, they do to a limited extent. You are entitled to an itemized deduction for all medical expenses you incur, including the cost of health insurance. However, you only get a tax benefit if you itemize your deductions, and then only to the extent your medical expenses exceed 7.5 percent of your adjusted gross income.

How would you like to almost double the tax savings presented in this example? You can. All you need to do is let your business pay for and deduct all your medical expenses.

Without getting into all the gory details, this deduction probably doesn't do you much good, if any. However, if you are self-employed you can deduct a portion of your health insurance even if you don't itemize.

As of 1995, the portion you will be able to deduct is 30 percent of your health insurance premiums.

These deductions help a little, but only a very little. For example, let's say you pay $200 each month for your family's health insurance and an additional $1,000 a year for out-of-pocket medical expenses. Given our basic assumptions of paying a combined federal and state income tax of 33 percent, your tax savings on your total medical expenses of $3,400 would be only $237.60.

How would you like to almost double the tax savings presented in this example?

You can. All you need to do is let your business pay for and deduct all your medical expenses. By making it a business expense you will be able to deduct 100 percent of it. And, what's more, the deduction will reduce not only your income tax but your self-employment tax as well.

Here's how to do it:

Step One: Hire your spouse as an employee.

Step Two: Let the business pay for your spouse's health insurance. If the policy is for your husband, make sure the policy includes your husband's children (*your* children!) and your husband's spouse (that's you!)

If you're self-employed, your business cannot pay

for and deduct the cost of your health insurance. However, your business can pay for and deduct the cost of its employees' health insurance. What's more, that policy can include coverage for the employee's children and spouse. And, that cost will be a deduction for the business and will not be included in the employee's income. And, the employee covered can be your spouse, even if your spouse is your only employee.

Step Three: Adopt a written medical reimbursement plan for your business. (Please see Appendix C for a Sample Plan.)

The effect of Step 3 is that all your employee's uninsured medical expenses (up to $5,000) will be paid for and deducted by your business. And, it will not be included in your employee's income. Since your spouse is an employee, this covers your whole family—including you. Now, all your medical expenses, including the cost of health insurance are 100-percent deductible by your business.

WARNING! Even though the health insurance policy can discriminate against other employees, the medical reimbursement plan cannot. If you have other eligible employees, all medical reimbursement plans must cover them as well as your spouse.

CALCULATE
YOUR TAX SAVINGS

1. Health Insurance Premiums $_____

2. Out of Pocket Medical Expenses $_____

3. Total Medical Expenses (Line 1+Line 2) $_____

4. Your Federal Income Tax Rate   ._____

5. Your State Income Tax Rate   ._____

6. Your Self-Employment Tax Rate   .13_____

(Adjust if not all earnings are subject to self-employment tax. Please see note on page 22.)

7. Your Total Tax Rate (Lines 2+3+4)   ._____

8. Line 3 x Line 7 $_____

     If you do not use Itemized Deductions, skip to line 10.

9.   a. Total Medical Expenses (Line 3) $_____

    b. Adjusted Gross Inc. $_____ x.075 $_____

    c. Medical Itemized Deduction
       (Line 9a - Line 9b) $_____

10. Health Ins. Premium (Line 1) x .30 $_____

11. Line 9c + Line 10 $_____

12. Income Tax Rate (Line 4 + Line 5)   ._____

13. Line 11 x Line 12 $_____

14. YOUR TAX SAVINGS (Line 8 - Line 13) $_____

Retirement Plans for Your Spouse

O NE OF THE LATER chapters in this book is devoted exclusively to how retirement plans can give you BIG Tax Saving Deductions. However, we'll take a little time here to discuss how hiring your spouse can boost that deduction.

Basically, retirement plans allow you to put some of your income in a special account earmarked for your retirement. And, that money will not be taxed in the year you earned it. So, if you earn $20,000 in a given year and put $1,000 of it in your retirement account, you will only be taxed on $19,000. However, the amount you can put in your account is limited by the amount of money you earned. It is possible to increase the amount your spouse can put in his or her retirement account by hiring your spouse and paying them wages.

The IRA account is one type of retirement accounts you are probably already familiar with. The amount you can put into an IRA account is limited to the lesser of $2,000 or your earned income. If you earn more than $2,000 and your spouse is unemployed, the two of you in total can put up to $2,250 each year into your IRAs. That's a potential tax savings of $742, assuming your total income tax bracket is 33 percent.

That's not bad. However, if you hire your otherwise unemployed spouse, each of you may contribute $2,000 into each of your IRAs for a total tax savings of $1,320, which is an additional $578 tax savings. That's much better.

The other type of retirement plan is the SEP Plan. This retirement plan offers far greater tax saving opportunities than the IRA. You can contribute up to a maximum of 15 percent of your employees' wages, with a ceiling of $22,500—as opposed to the $2,000 IRA limit.

Even if you are unable to put more than $2,000 in your spouse's retirement account, it still pays to set up a SEP for your spouse. That's because IRAs only reduce your income tax, not self-employment tax.

However, contributions by your business to your spouse's SEP account give you a deduction that not only reduces your income tax, but your self-employment tax as well. What's more, your spouse doesn't include the contribution in his or her income.

CALCULATE YOUR TAX SAVINGS

1. Contribution to Spouse's
   Retirement Account $_____

2. Federal Income Tax Rate   ._____

3. State Income Tax Rate   ._____

4. Self-Employ. Tax Rate (put zero if IRA)   ._____

5. Total Tax Rate (Lines 2+3+4)   ._____

6. YOUR TAX SAVINGS (Line 1 x Line 5) $_____

As I will discuss in Chapter 7, the SEP Plan has one pitfall: if you have other employees and you do not want to contribute to their retirement fund, you might have to set up another type of SEP Plan called a Salary Reduction Plan. Under that arrangement, you cannot contribute as much as in a regular SEP, but it's still more than an IRA. For 1994, the limit was $8,728.

Other Tax Benefits from Hiring Your Spouse

THERE'S A TAX SAVING benefit afforded working parents who pay for child care during the work day. The amount of this tax saving benefit is determined by two factors—it's cost and each parent's earned income.

Increased child care credits:
If one of the parents does not have any earned income, you don't get the benefit. So, if your spouse is otherwise unemployed or has a very low earned income, it's possible to increase the child care credit by increasing your spouse's earned income.

Deducting business traveling costs:
Another benefit to hiring your spouse is that they can come with you on business trips and your business can pay their way. We will discuss this in Chapter 6, Tax Saving Deductions for Business Trips. You may take your spouse on a business trip and deduct your spouse's and your expenses.

WATCHOUT! If your earned income already exceeds the self-employment/FICA tax ceiling ($57,600 for 1994), it might not be to your advantage to hire your spouse. Check with your tax advisor for details.

Helpful Hints for Hiring Your Child or Spouse

L ET'S FACE IT, HIRING a family member can save you a lot in taxes—so naturally the IRS figures that means there might be a temptation to take advantage of these tax saving deductions without your family member doing any real work for you. Therefore, you must be prepared during an audit to prove you are entitled to the deduction.

You must be able to substantiate that the amount you paid your family member was for services actually rendered, and that the amount you paid them was reasonable for the job they did.

The IRS would probably raise an eyebrow or two if you pay your fourteen-year-old son $20,000 a year to sweep the floors once a week.

However, keep in mind that your spouse and children may be already doing things for your business to help out. Cleaning the office, errands, stuffing envelopes, making bank deposits, answering the phone, and delivering packages are all legitimate examples of duties eligible for compensation.

Here's what to do:

1. **Make a written employment agreement between your business and your family employee. The agreement should contain a description of the services to be rendered, the amount of compensation, the fringe benefits, when the agreement begins and when it ends, and you should both sign it. (Please see the sample employment agreement printed in Appendix B.)**

2. Make sure they fill out required employment forms such as Forms W-4 (see Appendix F) and I-9.

3. Provide them and the government with *timely* filed W-2s.

4. File all other employment-related forms with federal, state, and local governments in a *timely* manner.

5. Make sure they fill out time cards.

6. Pay them at regular intervals and on time.

7. Make sure they qualify as employees and not as independent contractors. (See the chapter on Independent Contractors Versus Employees).

☞ TAX SAVING ACTION STEPS YOU CAN TAKE TODAY

HIRE YOUR FAMILY MEMBERS

☑ Write an employment agreement. Make sure it contains:

A description of any services to be performed.

The amount of compensation.

The fringe benefits.

The time period the agreement covers.

Both you and the family member sign the agreement.

☑ Have the family member fill out a W-4 Form and a I-9 Form.

☑ Have the family member fill out time cards.

☑ Pay them at regular intervals and on time.

☑ File all government employee related documents in a timely manner.

SET UP A HEALTH CARE PLAN

☑ Hire your spouse.

☑ Have your business purchase a health insurance policy on behalf of your spouse and all your spouse's family, including you.

☑ Adopt a medical reimbursement plan for your business. Make sure it's in writing. (Please see the sample printed in Appendix B.)

SCORECARD

Tax Saving Strategy	Ease of Implementation	Tax Saving Benefits
	3 - easy to implement 2 - average to implement 1 - difficult to implement	3 - save lots of $ 2 - save some $ 1 - save little $
Hire your child(ren)		
Hire your spouse		
Purchase health insurance for your employee spouse		
Adopt a medical reimbursement plan		
Set-up a retirement plan for your employee spouse		

Chapter 5

THE "3- MARTINI LUNCH" IS NOW THE "BURGER AND GLASS OF WATER LUNCH"

It used to be when you went out for a meal during the work day with a business associate, such as a client, you were allowed to deduct 100 percent of the cost of the meal, including drinks. It became known as the "Three-Martini Lunch."

IT SEEMED EVERYBODY was going out on business lunches and writing it off. Fancy restaurants loved it. They were packed during what would otherwise be a low-traffic part of the day. Then, the tax law was changed. The Three Martini Lunch became The 2.4 Martini Lunch. That's when the deduction for meals and entertainment became limited to 80 percent of its cost.

In and of itself, that wasn't too bad. However what qualified for the deduction was also drastically restricted. No longer were businesses willing to pay for extravagant lunches. Martinis became Perrier, and Filet Mignon got ground up into hamburgers. Many fancy restaurants that once prospered closed their doors and became fast food stands or pizza parlors.

And now, as of 1994, what was once The Three Martini Lunch has become the "I'll have a burger and a glass of water" lunch. That's because, as of January 1st, 1995, only 50 percent of the cost for business meals and entertainment is deductible.

When does a meal and entertainment qualify as a Tax Saving Deduction?

Not only has the law limited the amount we can deduct for entertainment (meals are considered a form of entertainment) to 50 percent of its cost, but the meals and entertainment that qualify for the deduction is also very limited.

To be deductible the entertainment must first be either:

1. Directly related or associated with the active conduct of your trade or business, or

2. Meals consumed while away from home overnight on business (see Chapter 6, Tax Saving Deductions For Business Trips).

Directly Related or Associated with the Active Conduct of Your Trade or Business: A meal or entertainment expense is considered directly related or associated with the active conduct of your trade or business only if you conduct a substantial and bona fide discussion related to the active conduct of your business either during, immediately before, or immediately after the entertainment.

"Immediately before or after" is not to be taken very literally. If the meal or entertainment takes place the same day as the discussion, it's considered immediate. If it's not the same day, that doesn't mean it's automatically disqualified. Instead, you consider all the facts and circumstances to determine if it qualifies or not.

By the way, IRS will not accept claims that a bona-fide business discussion took place during sporting events or country club visits, for instance.

For example, if the people you are entertaining arrive late at night and you take them to dinner, then meet with them the next day, the meal is considered as immediately preceding a business discussion and will therefore be deductible.

By the way, the IRS will not accept claims that a bona-fide business discussion took place during any activity where they consider no chance of engaging in the active conduct of business is possible. Such activities include sporting events, bowling, plays, country club visits, and vacation resort visits. What do you do in these circum-

65

stances? Make sure you have a qualifying business discussion immediately before or after.

What would you deduct in the following situation? Let's say you take your best customer out to dinner. He brings along his wife and best friend and your spouse comes, too. During the meal, a discussion takes place that qualifies as a business discussion. At the end of the meal you graciously pick up the tab. Can you deduct the whole tab?

No. The person for whom the expenditure was made must engage with you in the active conduct of your business. However, expenditures for spouses of qualifying persons are deductible. In our example you can deduct for the portion of the bill related to your customer, his wife, your spouse, and yourself—but not the friend.

And how much is deductible? Only 50 percent of the qualifying amount.

Tips to go along with the main dis-course:

🖎**TIP** If you want to take your client or other business associate to a football game or other form of entertainment, make sure you have a business discussion with them some time during that day.

🖎**TIP** Here's how to get around the 50 percent limitation. Instead of going with your client to the football game or restaurant, give them the entertainment or meal as a gift. Pay for their entertainment, but don't tag along.

Gifts are 100-percent deductible. However, gifts to individuals are limited to $25 per donee per year. But, guess what? Gifts to non-individuals, such as corporations and partnerships, are 100-percent deductible without a cap. Just make sure the gift does not clearly benefit any particular individual.

What do you do if you've already given a $25 gift to your best customer and he's back in town? You can still pay for his entertainment, only this time you can tag along and get a deduction for business-related meal and entertainment expenses. The deduction will be limited to 50 percent, but that's better than nothing.

Remember, substantiation IS required!

As with everything else we discuss in this book, whatever you deduct make sure you are able to substantiate. For all deductions for meals and entertainment, record the following information:

1. The cost of every expense. If a particular expense exceeds $25, you must also have documentation, such as a receipt. (For expenses where receipts are not usually provided, such as taxis, buses, tips, receipts are not required).

2. The date of the meal or entertainment.

3. The name, location, and type of entertainment.

4. When and where the discussion took place, how long it lasted, and who participated in it.

For gifts, you must substantiate:

1. The cost.

2. The date you gave the gift.

3. A description of the gift.

4. The business reason for the gift or the value of the business benefit to be derived or expected to be derived as a result of the gift.

5. The occupation or other information related to the recipient, such as the recipient's name and title. The point here is that you must show a business relationship.

SCORECARD

Tax Saving Strategy	Ease of Implementation	Tax Saving Benefits
	3 - easy to implement 2 - average to implement 1 - difficult to implement	3 - save lots of $ 2 - save some $ 1 - save little $
Keep meal & entertainment log		
Convert 50% deductible entertainment expenses into 100% deductible gifts		

Chapter 6

TAX SAVING DEDUCTIONS FROM BUSINESS TRIPS

H ERE'S A POP QUIZ FROM the chapter on meals and entertainment. Let's say your spouse works for your business. One night, after closing a large deal, you celebrate. You go to a fancy restaurant specializing in French Cuisine and treat yourselves to the best wine in the house. You don't have any kind of business discussion. Do you think the IRS would challenge it if you took it as a deduction?

They sure would and you'd lose.

But let's take the same scenario and change the facts slightly. Let's say you're from L.A. and you close the deal in New York and then you go out to eat. Is the meal deductible? Same food, same wine, same discussion, same price. And a different outcome—this time it's deductible. What's the difference? In the second case you're away from home, while in the first case you're in your home town. Make sense? No. But then again why should it? After all, it's the Tax Law we're dealing with.

When you go away on business, you want to play your cards right to get the biggest Tax Saving Deductions possible.

If you do play your cards right, you can even turn your vacation into a Tax Saving Deduction. Here's how it works.

First, you must be on a business trip. What makes a business trip a business trip? This is not a Zen Koan. There are very specific criteria that must be satisfied. First of all, you must be away from home. Secondly, you must be away from home overnight. Well, that seems straight forward enough, doesn't it? (Don't forget we're dealing with the Tax Code.)

Home. Isn't that the place I come to after work to kick back on the ol' recliner, crack open a beer, and zone out on the tube? Not necessarily. For the purposes of this discussion, and to avoid confusion, we'll refer to your home as your "tax home."

Your tax home is where your regular or principal place of business is located. If you don't have a regular or principal place of business, your tax home will be your residence. I know that seems like an unnecessary distinction, but not everyone's residence is in the same place as their work.

For example, many Californians have taken refuge in Colorado—there are fewer people, lower taxes, and a much lower cost of living. Some of the Californians, however, don't want to leave their jobs or they can't find comparable work in Colorado. So they stay and work in California during the week and return home to Colorado on the weekends. Some even make enough money to commute between California and Colorado daily. For these people, Colorado is their home, but California is their tax home.

Let's put this definition into operation. If your residence and your primary place of business are in the same area, that's where your tax home is. If they're in different locations, your tax home is where you work.

What if you work in California and live in Colorado? Are the traveling costs between those two locations deductible? No, because that's commuting expenses—if you recall, transportation expenses between where you live and where you work are not deductible. But, what if, besides California being your principal place of work, you also conducted your business in Colorado? You still aren't entitled to a deduction for the cost of travel *unless* your primary motivation for traveling is business related.

If you do have two or more places of work, how do you determine your tax home? There are several factors to consider. The most significant is time spent in each location. The other two factors are the degree of business activity conducted in each place, and the relative significance of the financial return from each area.

By the way, does everyone have a tax home?

How about the salesman who travels all around the country and doesn't have a place he calls home. He sleeps in motels and eats in restaurants throughout the country. Since he doesn't have a regular or principal place of business, or a residence, he doesn't have a tax home and therefore cannot qualify for this deduction—he doesn't have a tax home to be away from. (However, he can still deduct for use of the car.)

It's time to get away from home and move on to the "overnight" part of the qualification. This term is a bit easier to define. If you're away from home substantially longer than an ordinary work day, and while away from home you need a substantial amount of sleep, you are considered to be away overnight. In most situations, if you're away from home for at least one night, you meet this qualification.

Don't forget, even if you don't meet this criteria, you can still deduct transportation expenses to and from temporary work locations outside of your normal geographical area of work. (Please see Chapter 3, Getting the Most "TSPM" Out of Your Car.)

Which Travel-Related Expenses Are Deductible?

HERE'S THE FUN PART. IF your business-related trip qualifies as taking you away from home overnight, you may deduct all ordinary, necessary, and reasonable expenses related to your trip. That includes the transportation costs from your door to your destination and back. It also includes incidental costs while getting there and back, such as food and lodging. Once at your destination it includes your lodging, food, drinks, taxi, bus fare, car rental, laundry, and even dry cleaning.

How much is deductible?

Once you've determined that the business trip is away from home overnight and the expenses are deductible, next you have to determine how much of that expense is deductible. Did you think if you spent one day of your trip on business and the other ten days playing in the ocean you could deduct the whole trip? That's a different kind of trip.

As with everything else, to determine the amount of your deduction, it's necessary to allocate your trip between the portion that's for business and the portion that was personal. If it's 100-percent business, it's fully deductible. How you determine the allocation percentage depends on whether you're traveling within the country or to foreign lands.

Traveling within the United States: If you're traveling within the country, and if you're primarily on business, your transportation expenses to and from your destination are 100-percent deductible. You read me right. That means if you leave Minnesota on business in the midst of a cold and snowy winter and travel to sunny, warm Florida, your airfare is deductible even if you work Monday through Friday and play golf on the weekend. However, if the trip if primarily personal in nature, the transportation costs are not deductible at all.

What about other expenses while you're in Florida? If the trip is primarily business, you may allocate the percentage of the total trip that is business related. If the trip is primarily personal, the only deductible expenses are those directly related to your trade or business.

☞ **TIP** Isn't it a drag to travel to a beautiful part of the country, be cooped up in an office Monday through Friday, then catch a late night flight home on Friday? Wouldn't it be nice to be able to spend at least one day taking in the sights? Well, you can. Plus you can even deduct the expenses of your meals and lodging for that extra day. If you're on a business trip and you extend the trip to over Saturday night, the Saturday will also be considered a business day and all the meals and lodging for that day will be deductible—IF by staying over a Saturday night you receive reduced airfares and your net overall costs are less than had you not stayed.

Foreign travels: Once again we have to divide the expenses of your traveling into two categories: First, the traveling costs you incur while en route to and from your destination and, second, the expenses you incur while at your destination.

The expenses you incur while going to and from your destination are not deductible at all if the trip is primarily personal. If the trip is primarily business, the business portion is deductible. However, you can deduct 100 percent of these expenses IF the trip is primarily for business AND you satisfy any one of the following three criteria.

1. The trip is for less than eight days, or

2. Less than 25 percent of the total days are non-business, or

3. Personal vacation is not a primary consideration on the trip.

Determining the Primary Purpose of the Trip

To determine whether the primary purpose of a trip is business or personal, consider all the facts and circumstances. The most important factor is the time spent at each. Generally speaking, a day is considered a business day if more than one half of the normal eight-hour work day is spent working. When it comes to your travels outside the country, any of the following will be considered business days:

 * Traveling days en route to your destination or going back home.

 * Days you attend a business meeting.

 * Any day in which your principal activity was business related.

That means if you fly to Paris and spend four additional days on business and seven days vacationing, your trip will be considered primarily personal and none of your transportation costs will be deductible. However, let's say that instead of flying to Paris you take a six-day cruise. As long as the cruise doesn't stop along the way for a non-business diversion, the trip will be considered primarily for business and ten seventeenths (that's 10/17) of the transportation expenses will be deductible.

Substantiation: Well, we once again address the topic most of us like even less than taxes—keeping records. When you're traveling, be sure to record the following:

1. The amount of each expense.

2. The dates of departure and return for each trip away from home, including days away from home spent on business.

3. **Where you went.**

4. **The business reasons or nature of the business benefit derived or expected to be derived as a result of the travel.**

You also need the receipts for items costing $25 or more, unless they're not readily available, such as for telephone, tips, and cabs. If you don't have a receipt, be sure you make a record of the expense anyway.

As a self-employed taxpayer you may elect to use standard per diem rates for meals and incidental expenses. The advantage of using the standard rates is you don't need receipts to prove these expenses. If your actual costs for meals and incidentals, such as the cost of laundry, cleaning and maid tips, are less than the standard per diem rate you definitely want to use the standard rates.

For 1994, the per diem rate was $26 each day in most areas of the country. For certain specified areas in the country, the rate may be $30, $34, or $38 depending on where you travel. (Please see Appendix E for locations eligible for higher allowances.) For locations outside continental USA, the rates are updated monthly. Call (703) 875-7910 for specific information.

Take Your Spouse with You

I F YOUR SPOUSE, OR for that matter anyone else, is your employee and you can find any legitimate business purpose for that person to go on the trip with you, your business can pay for and deduct that other person's expenses as well as your own.

BY THE WAY: What if your non-employee spouse goes with you? His or her expenses are not deductible.

Does that mean that if a single room costs $60 a night and a double costs $72 that you can only deduct $36 for the night? No, you still get to deduct the amount you would have been entitled to if you were alone. In this case, you may still deduct $60 a night for lodging.

Don't forget that if you have a legitimate business entertainment, the cost of your spouse is deductible—if you entertain clients while away on business and bring your spouse along, you will still be able to deduct your spouse's share of the entertainment.

Turning Your Vacation Into a Tax Saving Deduction

Y OU'VE WORKED THE WHOLE year. Now you're ready to unravel, relax, and let yourself wind down. It's time to go on your vacation. Instead of winding down and relaxing, you get more uptight because of the cost. You need to get away, but you can't really afford it.

If you play your cards right, you can have your cake and eat it, too. That is, you can go on your vacation at a reduced rate by turning your vacation into a Tax Saving Deduction, and let Uncle Sam pay for part of the trip. Here's how it works. Go to a place where you can conduct your business in some way. Spend four hours a day in places that in some way can be connected to your business, and do something business related. Make business contacts. Hand out and collect business cards. Record what you discussed and with whom. If possible, show what income you generated or in what ways your business derived a benefit from the trip.

Remember, if you bring along your spouse or child, be sure they are employees and have a business purpose for accompanying you on the trip so you can deduct the cost of taking them with you.

SCORECARD

Tax Saving Strategy	Ease of Implementation	Tax Saving Benefits
	3 - easy 2 - average 1 - difficult	3 - save lots of $ 2 - save some $ 1 - save little $
Set-up trips "primarily for business"		
Set-up foreign business trips for 100% deductible		
For business trips consider the standard meal allowance		
Take your employee spouse along		
Turn your vacation into a Tax Saving Deduction		

Chapter 7

RETIREMENT PLANS FOR THE SELF EMPLOYED

This section isn't for everyone. It's only for those who have enough money to put some in savings and that don't need to touch it until they're at least 59 and one-half years old. Most financial planners will advise you to not rely on social security alone, and to do everything you can to provide for your future.

I F YOU CAN AFFORD TO PUT money in savings, more than likely you'll want to put it into a retirement plan. Not only will you not have to pay tax on the amount you sock away in the year you sock it away, but the amount it earns each year will not be taxed until you withdraw it. This could amount to a good-sized nest egg by the time you retire.

RULE OF 72

You may use the Rule of 72 to determine how long it will take for your principal to double. You don't need to be a genius in calculus or have a fancy computer. All you need to do is divide 72 by your assumed rate of return.

For example, if you put $5,000 away in your retirement plan and you earn interest at a rate of six percent, the $5,000 will become $10,000 in 12 years (72 divided by 6 equals 12). By comparison, if you paid taxes on that money in the year it was earned, the same $5,000, assuming an effective 46-percent tax rate, would take over 20 years to reach the $10,000 level. That's because 46 percent of the interest earned would end up in the U.S. Treasury.

An Overview of Retirement Plans

B EFORE GETTING INTO THE nitty gritty of this topic, I want you to know that this is one of the most complex areas of our already very difficult to understand tax code. I will attempt to keep it basic, simple, easy to understand, and practical so you can apply it to your own situation.

Of the several types of retirement plans, there are only two that apply to the vast majority of self-employed taxpayers—IRAs and SEP plans. Most of you are already familiar with IRAs, but few are familiar with SEPs.

The other types of retirement plans fall under the headings Keogh Plans and 401(k) Plans. However, there are very few self-employed individuals who would benefit from these plans. Although there are some added features to the Keogh arrangement or 401(k) Plans, they are very complex, require a lot of paperwork, and end up being quite costly to put into operation.

Individual Retirement Accounts (IRAs)

L ET'S START OFF WITH IRAS. If you like to do things the easy way, it doesn't get any easier than this. All you have to do is go down to the bank or an investment broker and tell them you want to set up an IRA. They'll give you a couple of short forms to fill out and that's that. You don't have to file anything with the IRS, and you don't need permission from your employees. Each year you deposit up to $2,000 before April 15th.

The basics are that you can make a tax deductible contribution to your IRA each year for an amount equal to the lesser of $2,000 or your earned income. If your business turns a profit of $40,000 you can contribute up to $2,000. If your business turns a profit of $1,500 and it's your only taxable compensation, you may contribute up to $1500.

If your spouse is unemployed and you file a joint return, the upper $2,000 limit becomes $2,250.

☟**TIP** Don't forget that you can hire your spouse. If you do, you are each entitled to make a contribution of up to $2,000. Assuming your state and federal income tax bracket totals 33 percent, you save one-third the amount you put into your IRA. If you contribute $2,000, you save $666. If you and your spouse each contribute $2,000, you save $1,333.

🖎 **TIP** If you do not have enough money to put into your IRA, but you will be receiving a tax refund, here's what to do. File your tax return early and claim a deduction for an IRA contribution. You do not have to make the contribution until the due date of the tax return, April 15th. If you file early enough, you will receive the refund before the due date and you can then use that refund for your IRA deposit. Just make sure you deposit it by April 15th.

WARNING! If you *or your spouse* is an active participant in certain other retirement plans, the amount of your tax deductible contribution may be limited.

SEP Plans

NOW, LET'S GET INTO SEP PLANS so I can show you how to save big bucks. SEP plans stand for Simplified Employee Pension plans. On a rating of one to ten as to simplicity of setting up, if the IRA is a 10, the SEP is a 9.5—it's not as simple as an IRA, but it's still easy. Just go down to your bank or investment broker and they'll show you what to do. There is a special IRS form to fill out (Form 5305-SEP; please see Appendix G), but that doesn't even need to be filed with the IRS (the bank just keeps it on file).

A SEP plan is similar to an IRA, however it can afford you much greater tax savings. Assuming an effective federal and state income tax rate of 33 percent, the maximum tax savings you can derive from an IRA is $660 (33 percent of $2,000). Under a SEP plan, given the same tax bracket, you can save as much as $6,456. That's a huge difference, making it more than worth your while to explore its possibilities.

There are two kinds of SEP plans, an ordinary SEP and a Salary Reduction Plan.

Under an ordinary SEP plan, your contribution depends on the percent of profit you elect to contribute and the amount of your profit. However, if it's your business, you can't contribute more than 13.0435 percent of your profits, with a profit ceiling of $150,000. This comes to a maximum contribution to your own SEP account of $22,500. (By the way, you can contribute 15 percent to your employees' SEP Plan. If you are self employed, the 13.0435 percent is derived from the 15 percent via a complicated and bizarre formula.)

The major drawback to an ordinary SEP plan is that all eligible employees must participate in the plan. Eligible employees are those that are 21 or older, who earned more than $395 for that year, and who have worked during three out of the last five years.

Obviously, if you have no employees other than your spouse who qualify, this is not a problem. If it is a problem, you can use the Salary Reduction SEP plan. The key difference between this kind of retirement plan and the ordinary SEP is the ordinary SEP contribution is made by the business in addition to your employee's salary. Under the Salary Reduction plan, as its name implies, the contribution is actually taken out of the employees' wages. It doesn't cost you anything extra. However, the potential tax saving benefits aren't as great, either.

The maximum contribution allowed under this plan is adjusted annually by the IRS. For 1994, the limit was $9,240. To implement this plan, you may not have more than 25 employees and half of all your eligible (as defined above) employees must agree with the plan. Also, the contribution to your personal plan, as well as to all other highly-compensated employees, cannot exceed 125 percent of the average contribution made to all other employees.

As I mentioned before, the advantage of this plan is that it doesn't cost you anything extra, and it still gives you a greater deduction than the IRA—though not as much as an ordinary SEP.

Now, I'm not encouraging anyone to be a tight wad with their employees, but the fact of the matter is most small businesses don't have the luxury to give their employees this kind of a benefit and stay alive.

NOTE: If 15 percent of your earned income comes out to be less than $2,000, you can still contribute up to $2,000 to your IRA account.

CALCULATE
YOUR TAX SAVINGS

1. Contributions To Your Retirement Plans $_____

2. Income Tax Rates:

    a. Federal Income Tax Rate   ._____

    b. State Income Tax Rate   ._____

    c. Total Income Tax Rate (Line 2a + 2b)   ._____

3. Your Tax Savings (Line 1 x Line 2c) $_____

⤷**TIP** As you probably know, if you withdraw money from your IRA or SEP before you reach the age of 59 and one-half, you will be subject to a ten-percent tax in addition to paying income tax on the amount of your withdrawal. If you wait till after the age of 59 and one-half, the amount you withdraw will be subject only to income tax and no penalty.

What you probably *don't* know is that there are times when it may pay for you to make an early withdrawal.

Let's say in a particular year your taxable income is reduced to zero. You decided to take a year off from work and travel the world. Or, perhaps your business had a bad year and suffered a loss. In those situations, if you withdraw funds from your retirement account, even though it will be subject to the ten-percent penalty, you might not have to pay income tax on it. In that case it's possible you'll have an overall tax savings by withdrawing it in a year that your tax rate is lower than usual. However, before taking advantage of this keep in mind that you might want to keep this money set aside as a nest egg for your retirement years.

NOTE: Although, Keogh and 401(k) Plans are complicated, expensive, and time consuming to set up and maintain there are some major benefits to them over an IRA or SEP. IF you are in a position to put more than 15 percent of your earnings into savings, or have employees and neither of the SEP plans fill your needs, there MIGHT be a Keogh or 401(k) plan for you. In that case consult your attorney. But, if you are like most self-employed individuals and you won't be contributing more than 15 percent to your retirement plan and you have no other employees (except for family members) then keep your life simple and set up an IRA or SEP plan.

☞ TAX SAVING ACTION STEPS
YOU CAN TAKE TODAY

SET UP A RETIREMENT PLAN

☑ If you are single or married and your spouse *doesn't* work for you:

Approximate the amount of money you can afford to put into a retirement plan this year.

If it is $2,000 or less then open an IRA account.

If it is more than $2,000 and you do not have any employees adopt an ordinary SEP Plan and open an IRA account.

If it is more than $2,000 and you have employees determine whether you want to contribute to their retirement plan also.

If you do, then adopt an ordinary SEP Plan and open an IRA account.

If you do not, then adopt a Salary Reduction SEP Plan and open an IRA account.

☑ If you are your spouse *does* work for you:

If you do not have any other employees then adopt a SEP Plan and open an IRA account.

☑ If you do have other employees:

Determine whether you want to contribute to their retirement plan also.

If you do, adopt an ordinary SEP Plan and open an IRA account.

If you do not, adopt a Salary Reduction SEP Plan and open an IRA account.

SCORECARD

Tax Saving Strategy	Ease of Implementation	Tax Saving Benefits
	3 - easy to implement 2 - average to implement 1 - difficult to implement	3 - save lots of $ 2 - save some $ 1 - save little $
Set-up an IRA account		
Set-up an IRA for spouse		
Set-up a SEP Plan		
Set-up a SEP Plan for employee spouse		

Chapter 8

TAX SAVING YEAR-END STRATEGIES

It's the end of the year and suddenly you wake-up panic stricken because you realize you're going to have to pay a lot more in taxes than you want to. You call up your accountant and say, "It's probably too late, but isn't there anything I can do to reduce my tax bite?"

EVEN THOUGH IT'S BEST TO START putting tax saving strategies into action at the beginning of the year, there are still a few things you can do. For the most part, year-end tax strategies are a question of timing. That is, whether it's more advantageous for you to decrease your taxable income this year and increase next year's, or to increase this year's and decrease next year's.

You might be wondering, "What kind of a choice is that? Of course I want to decrease this year's." In most situations you are right, you are going to want to decrease this year's taxable income. However, that's not always the case. For instance, let's say this year your income took a dive. You had a real bad year. But, you also know that next year it will be a lot better. The result is that this year's tax bracket will be lower than next year's. Let's say this year you're in the 15-percent bracket and next year you expect to be in the 28-percent bracket. In that case you might want to move some of next year's taxable income into this year for it to be taxed at the lower rate.

The terminology for manipulating taxable income from year to year is accelerating and deferring income and expenses. When you accelerate an income or expense that means you move it to this year (income that would otherwise affect next year's taxable income). Deferring income and expenses items means putting off until next year what would otherwise apply to this year's tax return. By deferring income and accelerating expenses you're able to reduce this year's taxable income. By accelerating income and deferring expenses you increase this year's taxable income, but decrease next year's.

Choosing the Method of Accounting That's Right for You

MOST TAXPAYERS ARE EITHER using the cash or accrual method of accounting. You made the choice when you started your business. After the first year you may change methods, but it's another one of those complicated IRS processes that requires special accounting. I highly recommend against changing.

Here's the difference between the two stated in very simple terms. In the cash method, you include income in the year you actually get paid. And you include deductions in the year you actually pay for the expenses. Let's say on December 25, 1995, you go to the office supply store and purchase $25 worth of supplies. You pay for it with cash. It's deductible in 1995. If, on the other hand, you have the store put it on your tab and you pay the tab in January of 1996— it will then be a deduction for you in 1996.

Okay, but here's a little twist for you: Let's say you pay for the supplies with a credit card and you pay off the credit card in 1996. In which year do you use the cost of the supplies as a deduction?

If you said 1996, you're wrong. The right answer is 1995. What?! This must be a misprint! No, it isn't. Here's the rule: If you purchase something on the store's credit, it's deductible in the year you pay off the credit. But, if you purchase something using credit from a source other than the merchant, it's deductible in the year you purchased the item. What's the logic to this? When you receive credit from a source other than the merchant, it's as if your creditor gave you the money and you paid the merchant with the money. Get it? Oh well, nobody ever said the tax law was logical.

That's the cash method. Under the accrual method of running your business, income is declared in the year it's earned and the deductions are declared in the year they are incurred.

Using the above example, if you purchased and paid for the office supplies in December of 1995, it's deductible in that year. If you purchased the supplies

91

in December of 1995 and paid for it with credit that was paid off in 1996, it's still deductible in 1995. And that's regardless of whether it's the store's credit or a credit card.

So which method should you choose? The rule of thumb is that if you expect your business to show more accounts receivable than accounts payable, select the cash basis. If it's the other way around, select the accrual basis. (Note that some taxpayers, however, are required by law to be on the accrual basis, such as businesses with inventory.)

Once you choose, you can change—but you must get IRS permission, the interim accounting is difficult, and it's an all-around hassle. For most taxpayers, if you have a choice, cash is the way to go. The accounting is easier and most taxpayers have higher receivables than payables.

⇘**TIP** If you're a cash-basis taxpayer and want to have higher deductions this year, make your year-end purchases with cash (including checks) or credit cards.

⇘**TIP** If you want higher deductions this year, pay off your suppliers before the end of the year.

⇘**TIP** If you want lower income this year, hold off sending out invoices until the beginning of the following year.

⇘**TIP** If it's near the end of the year and you know you're going to purchase equipment in the near future, do it before the end of

the year. Although the purchase of equipment is usually depreciated over a number of years, you can deduct up to $17,500 of the purchase cost in the year of purchase.

AND BY THE WAY: What if on December 30th you pay all of 1996's rent? Do you get the entire deduction in 1995? No. Advance payments, for such expenses as rent, are only deductible within 12 months of when they're paid. But what if you paid for a year's rent on December 1st for December 1995 through November 1996? Then, you get to deduct the entire payment in 1995, even though it included most of 1996's rent. That's because the payment made doesn't extend beyond 12 months from when it was paid.

BY THE WAY AGAIN: This is for you, Mr. Attorney. You know all those disbursements you make on behalf of your clients? They can amount to a sizable chunk of change. Many attorneys were in the habit of deducting those expenses in the year they paid it, then included it as income when reimbursed by the client. Well, you can't do that anymore. The IRS is taking the position that if you expect to get reimbursed, the disbursements on behalf of your clients are treated as a loan and are therefore not deductible.

☞ TAX SAVING ACTION STEPS YOU CAN TAKE TODAY

IF TODAY IS NEAR THE END OF THE YEAR

☑ Purchase your supplies and equipment NOW instead of waiting until next year.

☑ Pay by cash, check, or credit card. Do not use the store's in-house credit plan.

☑ Pay off your suppliers before the end of the year. You do not have to wait for them to send an invoice, as long as you actually made the purchase before the end of the year.

☑ Do not send out invoices until the beginning of the following year.

SCORECARD

Tax Saving Strategy	Ease of Implementation	Tax Saving Benefits
	3 - easy to implement 2 - average to implement 1 - difficult to implement	3 - save lots of $ 2 - save some $ 1 - save little $
Year-end tax planning: Decide whether to decrease this year's taxable income and increase next year's, or decrease next year's and increase this years. Then implement the year-end Tax Saving Strategies that are in accord with that decision		

Chapter 9

IT PAYS TO CLASSIFY YOUR WORKERS AS INDEPENDENT CONTRACTORS, BUT BEWARE!

If you had a choice, would you hire someone as an employee or an independent contractor? Looking at the choice from a strictly financial angle, you'd probably prefer hiring an independent contractor. Why? Because it's cheaper.

I F YOU pay a worker $10 an hour to do a job, and the worker is classified as an independent contractor, you pay him $10 per hour. However, if the same worker is classified as an employee, it will cost you, on the average, 1.4 times the wage. A $10 per hour salary will typically cost you $14.

Here's why. When you hire someone as an employee, in addition to their wages, you also owe the employer's share of FICA, state and federal unemployment insurance, workers' compensation, and fringe benefits. For the average company, the additional costs amount to 40 percent of wages. And that doesn't include the clerical time and money it costs to prepare and submit all the necessary employment-related forms. Independent contractors, on the other hand, generally do not require any additional costs or paper work.

Earlier we discussed providing fringe benefits to family members and SEP retirement plans. I referred to the pitfall, in certain situations, of having to provide the same benefits to all your employees. You do not have to provide those or any other benefits to independent contractors.

Why Many Workers Prefer To Be Classified As Independent Contractors

A worker who's classified as an independent contractor has the benefit of offsetting his or her income with business-related expenses. While employees can do that too, independent contractors are afforded many advantages. For one, employees only get the deduction if they can itemize deductions—and even then there's a two percent of Adjusted Gross Income floor they need to exceed. Also, the independent contractor can deduct more types of expenses. The independent contractor's expenses serve to decrease his or her self-employment tax. For the employee, the business deduction only decreases income tax, not their FICA.

Here's an example to help illustrate the point. Let's say a single taxpayer earns $20,000 for the year as an employee. Assuming the taxpayer has no other income and doesn't itemize deductions, the federal tax would be $2,066 and the share of FICA would be $1,530. In addition you, the employer, would be responsible for the payroll taxes, for workers' compensation, and would have to include the employee in any fringe benefit plans you have set up.

On the other hand, if you hired the worker as an independent contractor, the worker is able to deduct any related business costs right off the top. The contractor might get a deduction for an office at home, the use of computers and a car, the cost of business-related workshops and seminars, and so on.

GENERAL RULE: The general rule for workers is this—if, as an independent contractor, the tax benefit they receive from their expenses exceeds their share of FICA tax (7.65 percent), it probably pays for them to be an independent contractor. (If you have independent contractors working for you, show them this book, as they can use these tax saving tips themselves.)

The two other considerations are whether there are any employee benefits they would be sacrificing and whether they could lose their eligibility for unemployment insurance.

The IRS Prefers Workers To Be Classified As Employees (Of Course)

IN MOST SITUATIONS WHERE there are two unrelated parties involved, the IRS does not get involved in determining their relationship to each other. Usually, the IRS lets stand how the parties want their relationship to be defined, because in most situations what benefits one party is a detriment to the other.

However, when it comes to classifying workers as employees or independent contractors, the IRS takes a very active role. In these cases of a worker's status, it is often a win-win-lose situation. That is, if the worker and employer elect to treat the worker as an independent contractor, the employer wins, the worker wins, and the IRS (and other government agencies) lose. The IRS isn't going to allow someone to be classified as a contractor, even if there is a written contract, unless the contractor meets some very stringent tests.

There is so much money at stake with this issue that the IRS has set up a special division whose job it is to investigate possible misclassifications. If you do mis-classify a worker, the penalties can get very expensive. And don't think the classification is safe just because you have a written agreement that clearly spells out that the worker is an independent contractor. The IRS will deem that document as self-serving, and will apply the "a rose by any other name is still a rose" test. If a worker looks like an employee, smells like an employee, and works like an employee, they're an employee no matter what your agreement is. So, read this chapter very, very carefully. It can save you lots of money, as well as lots of worry and aggravations.

The Factors

THE PRIMARY FACTOR THAT is taken into consideration in the classification of a worker is CONTROL. If the employer has the *right* to control and direct the worker, the worker is an employee.

As a recent IRS publication stated, "In a nutshell, if the person who employs you sets your work hours, provides you with tools, tells you what to do and how to do it, and can fire you, then chances are you're an employee...not an independent contractor."

I underscore the word *right* because I want to emphasize that even if the employer doesn't exercise actual control, as long as he has that right then the worker is an employee.

Here's a list of 20 factors, supplied by the IRS, to help you determine the status of a worker. The degree of importance of each factor varies depending on the type of work performed and the factual context in which the services are performed.

For each of the following 17 questions a "NO" response puts a check in the independent contractor column.

	YES	NO
1. Must the worker comply with the employer's instructions about when where or how to work?	☐	☐

	YES	NO
2. Does the worker receive employer sponsored training?	☐	☐
3. Does the worker provide services that are an integral part of the business?	☐	☐
4. Must the worker render services personally?	☐	☐
5. Does the worker hire, supervise, and pay assistants for the employer?	☐	☐
6 Does the worker have a continuing relationship with the employer?	☐	☐
7. Must the worker follow set hours of work?	☐	☐
8. Does the worker work full time for the employer?	☐	☐
9. Does the worker work on the employer's premises?	☐	☐
10. Does the worker perform tasks in an order of sequence set by the employer?	☐	☐
11. Must the worker submit oral or written reports?	☐	☐
12. Is the worker paid by hour, week, or month?	☐	☐
13. Is the worker paid for business and /or traveling expenses?	☐	☐
14. Is the worker furnished with tools and materials?	☐	☐
15. Does the worker work for only one employer at a time?	☐	☐
16. Can the worker be fired?	☐	☐
17. May the worker quit without incurring liability to the employer?	☐	☐

For each of the following 17 questions a "YES" response puts a check in the independent contractor column.

	YES	NO
18. Does the worker have a significant investment in the service-provided facilities?	☐	☐
19. Can the worker realize a profit or loss?	☐	☐
20. Does the worker make services available to the general public?	☐	☐

POP QUIZ: If you hire your spouse or other family member for the Tax Saving Benefits previously described do you want them to meet the qualifications of an independent contractor? NO! Make sure they qualify as employees or you'll lose most of the tax benefits you get from hiring them in the first place.

NOTE: In some cases a worker might be considered as an independent contractor for income tax purposes but not for Social Security purposes. That means the employer wouldn't have to withhold income taxes but would have to pay and withhold FICA (Social Security) taxes. One example is home workers who perform services on goods and materials provided by the business they are working for, such as workers who sew clothes at their home for a clothes manufacturer. A worker that performs this kind of work, even if they are self directed, will still be considered an employee. This rule also applies to certain drivers in the distribution of specified goods and services.

On the other hand, real estate sales people and direct sellers of consumer products are automatically considered as independent contractor for all purposes.

Safe Harbor

WHAT IF YOU'VE ALWAYS treated a particular worker as an independent contractor but, after reviewing the above list, you realize you have been classifying them wrong all these years? Should you freak-out and run to your nearest IRS office confessing your sins? Should you rush to change the worker's status as soon as possible? No! Calm down. There are Safe Harbor provisions in the tax code that might protect you.

If you have erroneously classified a worker as an independent contractor you will not have to worry about the past, and you will not even have to make the change for the future, if you had a reasonable basis for treating the worker as an independent contractor, *and* all the required federal information and employment tax forms filed are consistent with this basis, *and* you haven't treated any worker holding a similar position as an employee since the beginning of 1978.

The following are some of the grounds for reasonable basis:

➤ JUDICIAL OR IRS precedent

➤ PAST IRS AUDITS didn't yield any challenges

➤ LONG-STANDING, recognized practice by a significant segment of your industry.

103

NOTE: This safe harbor provision only applies to the IRS, not to state agencies.

What You Can Do

IF YOU TREAT someone as an independent contractor, make sure to:

➤ HAVE A SOLID AGREEMENT (please see the sample agreement printed in Appendix D)

➤ KEEP TO THE TERMS OF THE AGREEMENT

➤ MAKE SURE THE WORKER OPERATES LIKE A BUSINESS (for example, business cards, invoices, separate office, letterhead, license, business phone, listings, and so on)

➤ TREAT THE WORKER AS A BUSINESS

➤ FILE THE NECESSARY PAPERS (such as Form 1099-MISC).

There are two other methods that help solidify the independent contractor status, but remember, they are not foolproof. The first is to require your worker to incorporate and to hire and pay the corporation. Be sure to include "Inc." at the end of their name on the check and in your check register. Another method is to hire your workers through an employee leasing firm.

SCORECARD

Tax Saving Strategy	Ease of Implementation	Tax Saving Benefits
	3 - easy to implement 2 - average to implement 1 - difficult to implement	3 - save lots of $ 2 - save some $ 1 - save little $
If your workers qualify, hire them as independent contractors		

Chapter 10

OTHER IMPORTANT TAX SAVINGS

Child Care Expenses

IF YOU HAVE ANY CHILDREN UNDER the age of 13, you'll want to read this section. Expenses incurred for the care of your children while you are at work or on a business trip can be paid and deducted by your business. This applies to all child care related expenses, such as the cost of baby sitters, day camp, nursery schools, and domestic services at home for such things as laundry, cleaning and cooking. (Note: This deduction doesn't include the cost of sending your child to private elementary school.)

For your business to be entitled to this deduction, you are required to set up your company with a plan for paying for the cost of dependent care for your employees, including yourself. Make sure the plan is in writing. It must include all your employees, not just yourself. And, the owner's share of the child care benefits paid out cannot exceed 25 percent of the total child care benefits paid. The maximum the plan can pay each employee, without including the money as income to the employee, is $5,000 ($2,500 if married filing separate returns). The plan can cover the costs only for children under 13.

I know some of you are probably thinking of paying your children to take care of their brother or sister, aren't you? Sorry, but it won't work. Payments made to individuals who you can take a dependency exemption for, such as children under 19, are not eligible for this special deduction.

By the way, payments for the care of your children are eligible for a credit on your personal tax return. But, you can't have your cake and eat it to. You either have your business pay or you pay personally. In most situations, you will be better off paying it through your business.

☞ TAX SAVING ACTION STEPS YOU CAN TAKE TODAY

TURN YOUR CHILD CARE EXPENSES INTO A TAX SAVING DEDUCTION

☑ Have your business adopt a written dependent care plan. Please see the sample plan in the appendix.

☑ Remember, it must cover all your employees.

Scorecard

Tax Saving Strategy	Ease of Implementation	Tax Saving Benefits
	3 - easy to implement 2 - average to implement 1 - difficult to implement	3 - save lots of $ 2 - save some $ 1 - save little $
Adopt a written dependent care plan		

Getting the Biggest Tax Saving Deduction from the Interest You Pay and Paying the Least Taxes on the Interest You Earn

INTEREST DEDUCTIONS: Do you recall the good ol' days when you were able to deduct ALL your interest payments? It did not matter if it was interest on your home mortgage, or on your credit card, or on a loan from a bank. But now the interest is deductible only if on a home mortgage, certain investment interest situations, or a business-related expense.

So what do you think I'm going to advise you to do?

That's right. Now you're getting the hang of it—if you can, convert your personal loans to business loans.

And, as with all other deductions, a business deduction saves you more tax dollars than a personal deduction. That's because it also decreases your self-employment tax. So, even where you can deduct interest as an itemized deduction it would still be better as a business write-off.

 TIP Have a credit card that's used exclusively for your business. That way all finance charges and the annual fee will be deductible. Also, it will ease your bookkeeping task.

 ## TAX SAVING ACTION STEPS YOU CAN TAKE TODAY

CONVERT PERSONAL INTEREST INTO A A TAX SAVING DEDUCTION

☑ If you make some purchases on credit and some by cash or check:

☑ Credit purchases should be for business related expenses.

☑ If you have more than one credit card, designate one for business use and the other personal expenses. Pay off the personal one first.

Scorecard

Tax Saving Strategy	Ease of Implementation	Tax Saving Benefits
	3 - easy to implement 2 - average to implement 1 - difficult to implement	3 - save lots of $ 2 - save some $ 1 - save little $
Convert non-deductible personal interest expenses into a Tax Saving Deduction		

Interest Income: Since it's best for interest expense to be a business deduction, is it also better to include interest income as part of your business?

Surprisingly a lot of people make this mistake—they include interest income on their business tax return. If you put it on your Schedule C, it will not only be subject to income tax, but to self-employment tax as well. So make the IRS happy, DON'T include it as part of your business income.

Charitable Contributions

I'VE HAD MANY CLIENTS give me their Profit and Loss Statements and show me the bottom line, thinking that's what their business must pay taxes on. Not usually true. There are some adjustments to make to their financial statements.

I get some of the worst responses from my clients when I tell them charitable contributions are NOT an allowable deduction for their sole proprietorship, partnership, limited liability company, or S corporation. They can take it as a personal deduction IF they itemize, otherwise they will not receive a tax saving benefit from it.

Is there a way around this? Kind of. You must be able to come up with a legitimate business-related reason to reclassify the contribution as a deduction. For example, as I mentioned before, business-related gifts made to non-individuals are 100-percent deductible. Therefore, if you can classify the donation as a legitimate business gift, it will be deductible. This reclassification is more apt to escape a challenge if the charitable organization happens to be a good customer or client of yours and it's your standard practice to give gifts to your clients. Another way to do it would be to give them a special discount.

Deducting the Cost of Starting Your Business

W OULDN'T IT BE WONDERFUL if you could start your business and earn money without having to incur up-front costs? I couldn't even do that as a kid selling lemonade in front of my house. Before I was able to make my first sale I had to buy the ingredients, paper cups, and napkins. Lucky for me, I was able to use my mother's mixing bowl and ladle.

These up-front costs are, in general, referred to by the IRS as start-up costs. And, start-up costs, unlike most other categories of expenses, are not deductible in the year incurred. They're considered as part of your investment and therefore increase your basis in your business.

You can elect to deduct these expenses over a period of 60 months. I have yet to find anyone who didn't take this option. If you don't choose this option, the costs will increase your basis in the business and you will reap the Tax Saving Benefit of that expense only when you sell or go out of business. Most people would rather get the write-off over five years rather than waiting until later.

In fact, I'd bet you would rather get the full tax benefit of the expense in the year it's incurred rather than spreading it out over five years. One of the few times this will not be the case is if deducting all up-front costs in the first year produces a loss for the business. And, if the taxpayer doesn't have any other income for the loss to offset, it might be better to deduct the expenses in future years.

There are two ways you can get around the five-year amortization rule. One is to simply put off incurring as many of the start-up expenses as possible until after your business begins.

There is no single, clear rule as to what is considered the starting point for a business. Some cases have held that a business is deemed to begin at the time its doors are opened to the public, and others have held when the business makes its first sale. In other words, my lemonade business did not begin when I went to the grocery store to buy the ingredients. Nor did it begin while I was setting up the stand. It either began when a passerby *could* have made a purchase or when the first sale was in fact made.

The second way start-up costs are deductible is when you are expanding an already existing business. For example, after my lemonade business began I could have started expanding my line to chocolate chip cookies. Other illustrations would be a lawyer already in practice starting to give workshops related to his practice, or a restaurateur expanding into the catering market.

Start-up costs include expenses incurred for both investigating a prospective business and getting the business started.

The following are some examples of start-up costs: a survey of potential markets, advertisements placed prior to the start of your business, salaries and wages paid to employees while they are being trained, fees paid to their instructors, and travel to prospective distributors, suppliers and customers.

Research and experimental costs are excepted to the start-up cost rules and may be deducted, in full, in the year incurred.

Scorecard

Tax Saving Strategy	Ease of Implementation	Tax Saving Benefits
	3 - easy to implement 2 - average to implement 1 - difficult to implement	3 - save lots of $ 2 - save some $ 1 - save little $
If starting a business, convert start-up costs into a deduction for this year		
In year start business, elect to amortize start-up costs over 60 months.		

Chapter 11

A FEW LAST WORDS

Choosing the Right Tax Professional To Get the Most Out of This Book

T HIS BOOK CONTAINS THOUSANDS of dollars worth of Tax Saving Deductions. Most of the ideas presented can be implemented right away, without consulting a professional. But, to get the most tax saving benefits or to get help preparing their taxes, some people want to use a tax professional who can help apply these Tax Saving methods to their particular situations.

Tax professionals come in all different types and styles. There are accountants, CPAs, bookkeepers, lawyers, and other general business consultants. Some specialize in working with large corporations, others small businesses, and others with self-employed professionals.

Most take a conservative posture when dealing with your tax savings. They'll only give you tax savings advice that they know would never present a challenge from the IRS. And, they will steer you away from doing anything that might raise even the slightest eyebrow of a revenue agent. In most cases these advisers are covering their own butts. Under the tax law, tax professionals can be penalized if they improperly advise their clients or prepare tax returns for clients using inappropriate deductions, even if they're legal. They don't want to take the chance of the IRS coming after them.

But, it's you who lose out by not taking full advantage of every deduction allowable by law. You have more to gain by taking an aggressive stance.

First, when choosing a tax professional, get recommendations from friends and business associates and interview as many as you can until you find one that's right for you. It would be great if you could find a tax adviser who specializes in your industry. That is they have many clients in similar lines of work. If you're a real estate broker, try to find someone who works with a lot of other realtors.

Second, choose an adviser whose clients fit the size of your business. Tax Saving strategies are different for someone who makes a couple of hundred thousand dollars each year as opposed to a business whose net profit is under $50,000.

Third, pick a consultant whose philosophical approach to taxes, as to how conservative or aggressive they are, are in accordance with yours. However, keep in mind that you don't want to hire a "Yes" man. You want someone who you can bounce ideas back and forth with in order to arrive at creative solutions.

There's a difference between tax avoidance and tax evasion. Tax avoidance is perfectly legal. The courts have consistently held that there is nothing wrong with arranging your affairs so as to keep your taxes as low as possible. Tax evasion is a crime.

As the infamous Supreme Court Justice Learned Hand wrote, "Everybody does so, rich or poor; and all do right, for nobody owes any public duty to pay more than the law demands."

My recommendation is to pick an adviser who has your interest as his primary concern. And, your adviser should be willing to go as close to the line, that separates tax avoidance from tax evasion, as you feel comfortable with. However, your adviser should be knowledgeable enough to keep close to that line without crossing over to the tax evasion side. Afterall, you don't want to spend sleepless nights worrying about "getting caught."

The tools in this book can be maximized by showing the ones that you want to implement to your tax adviser. There are thousands of dollars worth of tax savings ideas in this book. You don't need to pay your adviser hundreds of dollars to learn them. Instead, you can spend a little time reviewing how they can best be applied to your situation.

The Step-By-Step Implementation Program

THROUGHOUT THIS BOOK I'VE given you Tax Saving Strategies potentially worth thousands of dollars every year. However, if you don't put them into action you will not benefit from them. For most people, it would be very difficult to implement all these strategies all at once. If you try to do too many at one time you'll probably get overwhelmed, put them on the back burner, and never get to any of them. That's why I set up this Step-by-Step Implementation Program.

By following this program you will, over time, reap the Tax Saving Benefits provided in this book.

Step 1: Fill-in the following **SCORECARD SUMMARY** from the scorecards you filled out at the end of each chapter.

Step 2: From the "Ease of Implementation" column, choose three of the Tax Saving strategies that you rated the highest score.

Step 3: For each of the next three weeks, put into action one of these three strategies. And remember the old adage, "Don't put off till tomorrow what you can do today." Start the first one today.

The reason to start with the easiest ones, even though they might not yield the greatest savings, is to get you on a roll. Once on a roll, you'll find it easier and easier to put into action the other Tax Saving Strategies.

Step 4: In the last column of the **SCORECARD SUMMARY** (marked "Total"), put the total score for that Tax Saving Strategy by adding together the two previous columns. Then pick the five Tax Saving Strategies that received the highest composite scores and create a time line for their implementation. It's important that the time line is reasonable. It's better for you to take a little longer implementing them, than for you to fall behind. If you do fall behind, adjust your plan and get back on track as soon as possible.

Step 5: After these five are implemented, set up a time line for the next five. Keep doing this until they are all implemented.

Step 6: You've probably saved thousands of dollars. Every year go back and look through the list to see what changes or additions to your plan you can make.

Scorecard

Tax Saving Strategy	Ch. #	Ease of Imple-menting	Tax Saving Benefit	T O T.
		3 - easy 2 - aver-age 1 - diffi-cult	3- save big $ 2 - save some 1 - save little	
Set-up a deductible office at your home				
Keep mileage log & record auto expenses				
Convert commuting non-deductible ex-penses into a Tax Saving Deduction				
Hire your child(ren)				
Hire your spouse				
Purchase health insur-ance for employee your spouse				

Tax Saving Strategy	Ch. #	Ease of Imple- menting	Tax Saving Benefit	T O T.
		3 - easy 2 - aver- age 1 - diffi- cult	3- save big $ 2 - save some 1 - save little	
Adopt a medical reim- bursement plan				
Set-up retirement plan for employee spouse				
Keep meal & enter- tainment log				
Convert 50% de- ductible entertainment expenses into 100% deductible gifts				
Set-up business trips so they are "primarily for business"				
Set-up foreign busi- ness trips so the ex- penses are 100% de- ductible				
For business trips consider the standard meal allowance				
Take your employee spouse along on busi- ness trips				

Tax Saving Strategy	Ch. #	Ease of Imple- menting	Tax Saving Benefit	T O T.
		3 - easy 2 - aver- age 1 - diffi- cult	3- save big $ 2 - save some 1 - save little	
Turn your vacation into a Tax Saving Deduc- tion				
Set-up an IRA account				
Set-up an IRA for spouse				
Set-up a SEP Plan				
Set-up a SEP Plan for employee spouse				
Year-end tax planning: Decide whether to de- crease this year's tax- able income and in- crease next year's; or, decrease next year's and increase this year's. Then, imple- ment the year-end Tax Strategies in accord with that decision				
If your workers qualify, hire them as inde- pendent contractors				

Tax Saving Strategy	Ch. #	Ease of Imple- menting	Tax Saving Benefit	T O T.
		3 - easy 2 - aver- age 1 - diffi- cult	3- save big $ 2 - save some 1 - save little	
Adopt a written de- pendent care plan				
Convert non- deductible personal interest expenses into a Tax Saving Deduc- tion				
If starting a business, convert start-up costs into a deduction for this year				
In year start business, elect to amortize start- up costs over 60 months				

APPENDICES

Appendix A: TAX RATE SCHEDULE FOR 1994

Single Individuals

If Taxable Income is:			
Over:	**But not over:**	**The tax is:**	**of the amount over**
$ 0	$ 22,750	0 + 15.0%	$ 0
22,750	55,100	3412.50 + 28.0%	22,750
55,100	115,000	12740.50 + 31.0%	55,100
115,000	250,000	31039.50 + 36.0%	115,000
250,000		79639.50 + 39.6%	250,000

Heads of Household

If Taxable Income is:			
Over:	**But not over:**	**The tax is:**	**of the amount over**
$ 0	$ 30,500	$ 0 + 15.0%	$ 0
30,500	78,700	4575.00 + 28.0%	30,500
78,700	127,500	18,071.00 + 31.0%	78,700
127,500	250,000	33,199.00 + 36.0%	127,500
250,000		77,299.00 + 39.6%	250,000

Married Filing Joint Returns

If Taxable Income is:			
Over	But not over:	The tax is:	of the amount over
$ 0	$ 38,000	$ 0 + 15.0%	$ 0
38,000	91,850	5,700.00 + 28.0%	38,000
91,850	140,000	20,778.00 + 31.0%	91,850
140,000	250,000	35,704.50 + 36.0%	140,000
250,000		75,304.50 + 39.6%	250,000

Married Filing Separate Returns

If Taxable Income is:			
Over	But not over	The tax is:	of the amount over
$ 0	$ 19,000	$ 0 + 15.0%	$ 0
19,000	45,925	2850.00 + 28.0%	19,000
45,925	70,000	10,389.00 + 31.0%	45,925
70,000	125,000	17,852.25 + 36.0%	70,000
125,000		37,652.25 + 39.6%	125,000

Appendix B

SAMPLE EMPLOYMENT CONTRACT

CAUTION: The following sample contract is intended to give the reader an illustration of an employment contract between a business and the business owner's spouse. It is for illustration purposes only and might not be suitable for your particular use. Before using this agreement, or any part of it, you should consult with your attorney.

This agreement dated _____, 19__ is made between _____ whose address is _____, hereinafter referred to as "Company", and _____ whose address is _____, hereinafter referred to as the "Employee".

The "Company" agrees to employ the "Employee" as a _____, and the "Employee" agrees to accept such employment in accordance with the following terms and conditions:

1. DUTIES OF THE "EMPLOYEE"

The duties of the employee shall be:

2. THE "EMPLOYEE'S" WORK HOURS

The "Employee's" typical work hours shall be ___ hours per week. Such hours of work shall be performed during "normal" working hours, unless otherwise agreed. "normal" working hours shall be from 9AM to 5PM, Monday through Friday.

3. TIME CARDS

The "Employee" is required to keep a time card on a daily basis and to submit it to the "Company" no later than _____ of the following week.

4. COMPENSATION

The "Employee's" compensation for work performed shall be $_____ per hour (or, a salary of $_____ per _____). The payments shall be made on the _____ day of each _____.

5. HOLIDAYS

The "Employee" shall be entitled to the following paid holidays:

6. VACATIONS

The "Employee" will be entitled to _____ paid vacation days per year, commencing after the first 6 months of employment.

7. HEALTH INSURANCE

The "Company" shall provide suitable health insurance for the "Employee". Such policy shall include coverage for the employee's spouse and dependent children.

8. MEDICAL REIMBURSEMENT

If the "Employee" qualifies, the "Company" agrees to include the "Employee" in its Medical Reimbursement Plan..

9. REIMBURSEMENTS

The "Employee" shall be reimbursed for all authorized expenses incurred on behalf of the "Company".

10. LENGTH OF EMPLOYMENT

The length of employment shall be from _____ 19___ to _____ 19___.

11. TERMINATION

Either party may terminate this agreement at any time. However, such termination must be preceded by written notice, at least 14 days prior to its effective date.

12. COMPLETE AGREEMENT

This agreement supersedes all prior agreements between the "Employee and the "Company" and may not be modified, changed or altered other than in writing and signed by both parties.

Both the "Employee" and the "Company" agree to the above terms.

_____

_____

Appendix C
SAMPLE MEDICAL REIMBURSEMENT PLAN

Note: The following Medical Reimbursement Plan is a sample and might not be applicable to your situation. Before adopting this plan, or any part of it, consult your attorney. If you decide to adopt a Medical Reimbursement Plan for your employees, in addition to this plan your company will also need a Plan Summary to be given to each participant and, if your company is a corporation, then minutes resolving to adopt the plan.

This Medical Reimbursement Plan, known as
_____(name of plan), was adopted by
_____ (company name), located at
_____ on this
date _____, 19___. Its effective date will
_____, 19___.

1. GENERAL INFORMATION

a. The Federal Employer Identification Number (FEIN) of the Plan's sponsor is:

b. The Plan number is:

c. The type of administration of the plan is:

d. The name, business address, and business telephone number of the Plan's Administrator and trustees (if any) are:

e. The employer will provide all contributions to the Plan.

f. December 31 shall be the end of the Plan's fiscal year.

2. WHO IS COVERED

The company shall reimburse "covered employees" for the "medical care" of that employee, the employee's spouse and their minor dependent children.

3. AMOUNT COVERED

The amount to be reimbursed shall be "medical expenses" in excess of the coverage provided by medical insurance. Such reimbursement shall not exceed $5,000 for each fiscal year.

4. MEDICAL CARE AND MEDICAL EXPENSES DEFINED

The terms "medical care" and "medical expenses" shall include only those medical costs incurred while the relevant employee was employed by the company. Also, the medical costs covered shall be limited to the kinds set forth in Section 213 of the Internal Revenue Code and its Regulations currently in effect or as may be amended.

5. COVERED EMPLOYEES

"Covered employees" shall include those employees who satisfy all of the following criterion:

A. Employees who meet the common law definition of an employee.

B. And has been employed for at least _____ months.

C. And has attained the age of _____.

NOTE: The following employees may be omitted:

a. Employees who have not worked for the company at least 3 years.

b. Employees who have not attained age 25.

c. Part-time or seasonal employees.

d. Certain employees included in a collective bargaining agreement.

e. Certain employees who are nonresident aliens.

6. TAX TREATMENT

It is intended that the benefits provided through this plan shall be deductible by the employer and excluded from the employees income.

7. TERMINATION OF PLAN

A. This plan or any of its provisions shall be terminated by:

1. The expiration of ten days from the date the company mails or posts notice   of the termination; or,

2. The bankruptcy, insolvency or winding up of the company; or,

3. The termination of a particular employee. In which case the termination of the plan will only apply to that employee.

B. Upon termination, an employee's benefits shall terminate and all benefits which would be owing, but are not yet claimed shall be _____(insert "paid" or "canceled").

C. Any prepaid benefit paid by the company shall be reimbursed by the employee.

8. GOVERNING LAW

This Plan shall be interpreted under the laws of the State of _____.

_____

company name

_____

owner's signature

Appendix D

SAMPLE INDEPENDENT CONTRACTOR AGREEMENT

Caution: The following sample contract is intended to give the reader an illustration of an agreement between a business and an independent contractor. It is for illustration purposes only and might not be suitable for your particular use. Before using this agreement, or any part of it, you should consult with your attorney.

AGREEMENT

Agreement is hereby made between the CLIENT and INDEPENDENT CONTRACTOR set forth below according to the following terms, conditions and provisions:

1. IDENTITY OF CLIENT

CLIENT is identified as follows:

Full legal name of CLIENT:_____.

Type of entity: [ ] Sole Proprietorship [ ] Partnership [ ] Corporation [ ] Other_____

Address:_____

Telephone Number: _____

2. IDENTITY OF INDEPENDENT CONTRACTOR

The independent contractor (hereafter "IC") is identified as follows :

Full legal name of
IC:_____

Type of entity: [ ] Sole Proprietorship [ ] Partnership [ ]
Corporation [ ] Other_____

Address:_____

Telephone Number: _____

Social Security No. or Federal E.I.N.

_____

3. JOB To Be Performed

CLIENT desires that IC perform, and IC agrees to perform, the following job:

_____

_____

_____

_____

4. TERMS OF PAYMENT

CLIENT shall pay IC according to the following terms and conditions:_____

_____

5. REIMBURSEMENT OF EXPENSES

CLIENT shall not be liable to IC for any expenses paid or incurred by "IC" unless otherwise agreed in writing.

6. EQUIPMENT, TOOLS, MATERIALS AND SUPPLIES

IC shall supply, at IC's sole expense, all equipment, tools, materials, and/or supplies to accomplish the job agreed to be performed.

7. FEDERAL, STATE AND LOCAL PAYROLL TAXES

Neither Federal, nor state, nor local income tax nor payroll tax of any kind shall be withheld or paid by CLIENT on behalf of IC or the employees of IC. IC shall not be treated as an employee with respect to the services performed hereunder for Federal or state tax purposes.

8. NOTICE TO IC REGARDING IC'S TAX DUTIES AND LIABILITIES

IC understands that IC is responsible to pay, according to law, IC's income tax. If IC is not a corporation, IC further understands that IC may be liable for self-employment (social security) tax, to be paid by IC according to law.

9. FRINGE BENEFITS

Because IC is engaged in IC's own independently established business, IC is not eligible for, and shall not participate in, any employee pension, health, or other fringe benefit plan, of the CLIENT.

10. CLIENT NOT RESPONSIBLE FOR WORKERS' COMPENSATION

No workers' compensation insurance shall be obtained by CLIENT concerning IC or the employees of IC. IC shall comply with the workers' compensation law concerning IC and the employees of IC, and shall provide to CLIENT a certificate of workers' compensation insurance.

11. TERM OF AGREEMENT

This agreement shall terminate at 11:59 p.m. on
_____, 199__.

12. TERMINATION WITHOUT CAUSE

Without cause, either party may terminate this agreement after giving 30 days prior written notice to the other of intent to terminate without cause. The parties shall deal with each other in good faith during the 30 day period after any notice of intent to terminate without cause has been given.

13. TERMINATION WITH CAUSE

With reasonable cause, either party may terminate this agreement effective immediately upon giving of written notice of termination with cause. Reasonable cause shall include:

A. Material violation of this agreement.

B. Any act exposing the other party to liability to others for personal injury or property damage.

14. NON-WAIVER

The failure of either party to exercise any of its rights under this agreement for a breach thereof shall not be deemed to be a waiver of such rights or a waiver of any subsequent breach.

15. NO AUTHORITY TO BIND CLIENT

IC has no authority to enter into contracts or agreements on behalf of CLIENT. This agreement does not create a partnership between the parties.

16. DECLARATION OF INDEPENDENT CONTRACTOR

IC declares that IC has complied with all Federal, state and local laws regarding business permits, certificates and licenses that may be required to carry out the work to be performed under this agreement.

17. HOW NOTICE SHALL BE GIVEN

Any notice given in connection with this agreement shall be given in writing and shall be delivered either by hand to the party or by certified mail, return receipt requested, to the party at the party's address stated herein. Any party may change its address stated herein by giving notice of the change in accordance with this paragraph.

18. ASSIGNABILITY

This agreement may be assigned, in whole or in part, by IC. IC shall provide written notice to CLIENT before any such assignment.

19. CHOICE OF LAW

Any dispute under this agreement, or related to this agreement, shall be decided in accordance with the laws of the State of _____.

20. ENTIRE AGREEMENT

This is the entire agreement of the parties.

21. SEVERABILITY

If any of this agreement is held unenforceable, the rest of this agreement will nevertheless remain in full force and effect.

22. AMENDMENTS

This agreement may be supplemented, amended or revised only in writing by agreement of the parties.

X_____

Date: _____

XYZ Client

X_____

Date: _____

ABC Independent Contractor

COMMENT: *This sample independent contractor agreement is taken from "The IRS, Independent Contractors and You!" by tax attorney and expert in this field James R. Urquhart III. He is a nationally recognized lecturer on the subject of independent contractors. Urquhart Business Seminars of 2061 Business Center Drive, Suite 112, Irvine, California 92715-1107 can be reached at 1-800-262-6554 (inside California call 1-800-826-3830). Of course an agreement alone will not create an independent contractor relationship if the factual basis is not there to support it.*

Appendix E

STANDARD MEAL ALLOWANCE CHART

KEY CITY[1]	COUNTY/LOCATION[1,3]	AMOUNT
ALABAMA		
Birmingham	Jefferson	$ 30
Hunstville	Madison	34
Mobile	Mobile	30
ARIZONA		
Grand Canyon Nat'l Park/Flagstaff	Coconino	30
Phoenix/Scottsdale	Maricopa	34
Prescott	Yavapai	30
Tucson	Pima; Davis-Monthan AFB	30
ARKANSAS		
Hot Springs	Garland	30
Little Rock	Pulaski	30
CALIFORNIA		
Bridgeport	Mono	34
Chico	Butte	34
Death Valley	Inyo	38
El Centro	Imperial	30
Eureka	Humboldt	30
Fresno	Fresno	34
Gualala/Point Arena	Mendocino	34
Los Angeles	Los Angeles, Kern, Orange & Ventura; Edwards AFB; China Lake Naval Center	38
Merced	Merced	34
Modesto	Stanislaus	34
Monterey	Monterey	34
Napa	Napa	34
Oakland	Alameda, Contra Costa, Marin	38
Ontario/Barstow/ Victorville	San Bernardino	34
Palm Springs	Riverside	38
Palo Alto/San Jose	Santa Clara	38
Redding	Shasta	34
Redwood City/San Mateo	San Mateo	34
Sacramento	Sacramento	34
San Diego	San Diego	38
San Francisco	San Francisco	38
San Luis Obispo	San Luis Obispo	38
Santa Barbara	Santa Barbara	34
Santa Cruz	Santa Cruz	34
Santa Rosa	Sonoma	34
South Lake Tahoe	El Dorado	38
Stockton	San Joaquin	30
Tahoe City	Placer	38
Vallejo	Solano	30
Visalia	Tulare	30
Yosemite Nat'l Park	Mariposa	38
Yuba City	Sutter	30
COLORADO		
Aspen	Pitkin	38
Boulder	Boulder	34
Denver	Denver, Adams, Arapahoe, Jefferson	38
Durango	La Plata	34
Glenwood Springs	Garfield	30
Grand Junction	Mesa	30
Keystone/Silverthorne	Summit	38
Steamboat Springs	Routt	30
Vail	Eagle	38
CONNECTICUT		
Bridgeport/Danbury	Fairfield	34
Hartford	Hartford, Middlesex	38
New Haven	New Haven	34
New London/Groton	New London	30
Salisbury	Litchfield	38
DELAWARE		
Lewes	Sussex	30
Wilmington	New Castle	34

KEY CITY[1]	COUNTY/LOCATION[1,3]	AMOUNT
DISTRICT of COLUMBIA		
Washington, DC	Virginia counties of Arlington, Loudoun, and Fairfax AND the cities of Alexandria, Fairfax, and Falls Church Maryland counties of Prince George's and Montgomery	$ 38
FLORIDA		
Cocoa Beach	Brevard	30
Fort Lauderdale	Broward	30
Fort Myers	Lee	34
Fort Pierce	Saint Lucie	30
Fort Walton Beach	Okaloosa	30
Gainesville	Alachua	30
Jacksonville	Duval; Naval Station Mayport	30
Key West	Monroe	38
Kissimmee	Osceola	30
Miami	Dade	34
Naples	Collier	34
Orlando	Orange	30
Panama City	Bay	30
Pensacola	Escambia	30
Punta Gorda	Charlotte	30
Saint Augustine	Saint Johns	30
Sarasota	Sarasota	30
Stuart	Martin	30
West Palm Beach	Palm Beach	34
GEORGIA		
Atlanta	Clayton, Cobb, De Kalb, Fulton	38
Norcross/Lawrenceville	Gwinnett	30
Savannah	Chatham	30
IDAHO		
Boise	Ada	30
Idaho Falls	Bonneville	30
Ketchum/Sun Valley	Blaine	38
McCall	Valley	30
Stanley	Custer	30
ILLINOIS		
Bloomington	McLean	30
Champaign/Urbana	Champaign	30
Chicago	Du Page, Cook, Lake	38
Peoria	Peoria	30
Rockford	Winnebago	30
Springfield	Sangamon	30
INDIANA		
Bloomington/Crane	Monroe, Martin	30
Columbus	Bartholomew	30
Evansville	Vanderburgh	30
Gary	Lake	30
Indianapolis	Marion; Fort Benjamin Harrison	34
Lafayette	Tippecanoe	30
South Bend	St. Joseph	30
IOWA		
Des Moines	Polk	30
Dubuque	Dubuque	30
Iowa City	Johnson	30
KANSAS		
Kansas City	Johnson, Wyandotte	34
Wichita	Sedgwick	30
KENTUCKY		
Bowling Green	Warren	30
Covington	Kenton	34
Florence	Boone	30
Lexington	Fayette	30
Louisville	Jefferson	34

139

KEY CITY[1]	COUNTY/LOCATION[2,3]	AMOUNT
LOUISIANA		
Alexandria	Rapides	$ 30
Baton Rouge	East Baton Rouge	30
Bossier City	Bossier	30
Lafayette	Lafayette	30
Lake Charles	Calcasieu	30
New Orleans	Jefferson, Orleans, Plaquemines, St. Bernard	34
Shreveport	Caddo	30
Slidell	St. Tammany	30
MAINE		
Auburn	Androscoggin	30
Bangor	Penobscot	30
Bar Harbor	Hancock	34
Kennebunk/Sanford	York	30
Kittery	Portsmouth Naval Shipyard	30
Portland	Cumberland	30
Rockport	Knox	30
Wiscasset	Lincoln	30
MARYLAND (See also District of Columbia)		
Annapolis	Anne Arundel	34
Baltimore	Baltimore, Harford	38
Columbia	Howard	34
Easton	Talbot	30
Frederick	Frederick	34
Hagerstown	Washington	30
Lusby	Calvert	34
Ocean City	Worcester	34
Salisbury	Wicomico	30
Tower Garden on Bay	Queen Anne's	30
Waldorf	Charles	30
MASSACHUSETTS		
Andover	Essex	34
Boston	Suffolk	38
Cambridge/Lowell	Middlesex	38
Hyannis	Barnstable	30
Martha's Vineyard/Nantucket	Dukes, Nantucket	38
Pittsfield	Berkshire	34
Quincy	Norfolk	34
Springfield	Hampden	30
MICHIGAN		
Ann Arbor	Washtenaw	30
Charlevoix	Charlevoix	30
Detroit	Wayne	38
Flint	Genesee	30
Grand Rapids	Kent	30
Kalamazoo	Kalamazoo	30
Mackinac Island	Mackinac	34
Port Huron	St. Clair	34
Saginaw	Saginaw	30
St. Joseph/Niles/Benton Harbor	Berrien	30
Traverse City	Grand Traverse	30
Troy/Pontiac	Oakland	34
MINNESOTA		
Bemidji	Beltrami	30
Brainerd	Crow Wing	30
Duluth	St. Louis	34
Grand Rapids	Itasca	30
Mendota Heights	Dakota	30
Minneapolis/St. Paul	Anoka, Hennepin, Ramsey; Detachment BRAVO at Fort Snelling, Rosemount	34
Rochester	Olmsted	30
St. Cloud	Stearns	30
MISSISSIPPI		
Biloxi/Bay St. Louis/Gulfport/Pascagoula	Harrison, Jackson, Hancock	30
Jackson	Hinds	30
Natchez	Adams	30
Ridgeland	Madison	38
Vicksburg	Warren	30
MISSOURI		
Branson	Taney	$ 30
Kansas City	Clay, Jackson, Platte	34
Lake Ozark	Miller	34
Osage Beach	Camden	30
Springfield	Greene	30
St. Louis	St. Charles, St. Louis	38
NEBRASKA		
Omaha	Douglas	30
NEVADA		
Las Vegas	Clark; Nellis AFB	38
Reno	Washoe	30
Stateline	Douglas	38
NEW HAMPSHIRE		
Conway	Carroll	30
Laconia	Belknap	30
Lebanon/Hanover	Grafton	34
Manchester	Hillsborough	30
Portsmouth/Newington	Rockingham; Pease AFB	30
NEW JERSEY		
Atlantic City	Atlantic	38
Belle Mead	Somerset	30
Camden	Camden	34
Edison	Middlesex	38
Freehold/Eatontown	Monmouth; Fort Monmouth	34
Millville	Cumberland	30
Moorestown	Burlington	34
Newark	Bergen, Essex, Hudson, Passaic, Union	38
Ocean City/Cape May	Cape May	34
Princeton/Trenton	Mercer	34
Tom's River	Ocean	30
NEW MEXICO		
Albuquerque	Bernalillo	34
Farmington	San Juan	30
Las Cruces/White Sands	Dona Ana	30
Los Alamos	Los Alamos	30
Santa Fe	Santa Fe	34
Taos	Taos	30
NEW YORK		
Albany	Albany	30
Binghampton	Broome	30
Buffalo	Erie	34
Corning	Steuben	30
Elmira	Chemung	30
Glens Falls	Warren	34
Ithaca	Tompkins	30
Jamestown	Chautauqua	30
Kingston	Ulster	30
Lake Placid	Essex	30
Monticello	Sullivan	30
New York City	Manhattan, Staten Island, Bronx, Brooklyn, Queens; Nassau, Suffolk	38
Niagara Falls	Niagara	34
Palisades/Nyack	Rockland	34
Plattsburgh	Clinton	30
Rochester	Monroe	34
Saratoga Springs	Saratoga	38
Schenectady	Schenectady	34
Syracuse	Onondaga	30
Troy	Rensselaer	30
Utica	Oneida	30
Watertown	Jefferson	30
West Point	Orange	34
White Plains	Westchester	38
NORTH CAROLINA		
Asheville	Buncombe	30
Charlotte	Mecklenburg	34
Duck	Dare	30
Greensboro/High Point	Guilford	30
Raleigh/Chapel Hill/Durham	Wake, Durham, Orange	34
Winston-Salem	Forsyth	30

140

KEY CITY[1]	COUNTY/LOCATION[2,3]	AMOUNT
NORTH DAKOTA		
Bismarck/Mandan	Burleigh, Morton	$ 30
Fargo	Cass	30
OHIO		
Akron	Summit	34
Cincinnati/Evendale	Hamilton, Warren	30
Cleveland	Cuyahoga	38
Columbus	Franklin	34
Dayton/Fairborn	Montgomery, Greene; Wright-Patterson AFB	30
Port Clinton/Oakharbor	Ottawa	30
Sandusky	Erie	30
Springfield	Clark	30
Toledo	Lucas	30
Warren	Trumbull	30
OKLAHOMA		
Norman	Cleveland	30
Tulsa/Bartlesville	Osage, Tulsa, Washington	30
OREGON		
Ashland/Medford	Jackson	30
Bend	Deschutes	30
Eugene	Lane	30
Lincoln City/Newport	Lincoln	30
Portland	Multnomah	30
PENNSYLVANIA		
Allentown	Lehigh	34
Bloomsburg	Columbia	30
Chester/Radnor	Delaware	38
Gettysburg	Adams	30
Harrisburg	Dauphin	34
King of Prussia/Ft. Washington	Montgomery	34
Lancaster	Lancaster	30
Mechanicsburg	Cumberland	30
Philadelphia	Philadelphia	34
Pittsburgh	Allegheny	34
Scranton	Lackawanna	30
Shippingport	Beaver	30
Somerset	Somerset	30
State College	Centre	30
Stroudsburg	Monroe	30
Valley Forge	Chester	38
Warminster	Bucks; Naval Air Center	30
Wilkes-Barre	Luzerne	30
York	York	30
RHODE ISLAND		
East Greenwich	Kent; Naval Construction Center in Davisville	34
Newport	Newport	38
Providence	Providence	34
SOUTH CAROLINA		
Charleston	Charleston, Berkeley	30
Columbia	Richland	30
Hilton Head	Beaufort	34
Myrtle Beach	Horry; Myrtle Beach AFB	30
TENNESSEE		
Gatlinburg	Sevier	30
Johnson City	Washington	30
Kingsport/Bristol	Sullivan	30
Knoxville	Knox; city of Oak Ridge	30
Memphis	Shelby	30
Nashville	Davidson	30
TEXAS		
Amarillo	Potter	30
Austin	Travis	34
Brownsville	Cameron	30
Corpus Christi/Ingelside	Nueces, San Patricio	30
TEXAS *(cont'd)*		
Dallas/Fort Worth	Dallas, Tarrant	$ 34
El Paso	El Paso	30
Galveston	Galveston	30
Houston	Harris; LBJ Space Center; Ellington AFB	38
Laredo	Webb	30
San Angelo	Tom Green	30
San Antonio	Bexar	30
UTAH		
Cedar City	Iron	30
Provo	Utah	30
Salt Lake City/Ogden	Salt Lake, Weber, Davis; Dugway Proving Ground; Tooele Army Depot	30
St. George	Washington	30
VERMONT		
Burlington	Chittenden	30
Middlebury	Addison	30
Rutland	Rutland	30
White River Junction	Windsor	30
VIRGINIA (See also District of Columbia)		
Charlottesville		34
Lynchburg		30
Norfolk/Virginia Beach/Portsmouth/Hampton/Newport News/Chesapeake	York; Naval Weapons Station, Yorktown	34
Richmond	Chesterfield, Henrico; Defense Supply Center	34
Roanoke	Roanoke	30
Warrenton/Amissville	Fauquier, Rappahonnock	30
Williamsburg		34
Wintergreen	Nelson	38
WASHINGTON		
Anacortes/Mt. Vernon	Skagit	30
Bellingham	Whatcom	30
Bremerton	Kitsap	30
Kelso/Longview	Cowlitz	30
Lynnwood/Everett	Snohomish	30
Port Angeles	Clallam	30
Richland	Benton	34
Seattle	King	34
Spokane	Spokane	30
Tacoma	Pierce	30
Tumwater/Olympia	Thurston	30
Vancouver	Clark	34
Whidbey Island	Island	30
Yakima	Yakima	30
WEST VIRGINIA		
Charleston	Kanawha	30
Martinsburg	Berkeley	30
Morgantown	Monongalia	30
Parkersburg	Wood	30
WISCONSIN		
Brookfield	Waukesha	34
Eau Claire	Eau Claire	30
La Crosse	La Crosse	30
Lake Geneva	Walworth	34
Madison	Dane	30
Milwaukee	Milwaukee	30
Oshkosh	Winnebago	30
Wisconsin Dells	Columbia	30
WYOMING		
Casper	Natrona	30
Cheyenne	Laramie	30
Jackson	Teton	34

Appendix F: IRS FORM W-4

Form W-4 (1995)

Want More Money in Your Paycheck?
If you expect to be able to take the earned income credit for 1995 and a child lives with you, you may be able to have part of the credit added to your take-home pay. For details, get Form W-5 from your employer.

Purpose. Complete Form W-4 so that your employer can withhold the correct amount of Federal income tax from your pay.

Exemption From Withholding. Read line 7 of the certificate below to see if you can claim exempt status. If exempt, complete line 7; but do not complete lines 5 and 6. No Federal income tax will be withheld from your pay. Your exemption is good for 1 year only. It expires February 15, 1996.

Note: You cannot claim exemption from withholding if (1) your income exceeds $650 and includes unearned income (e.g., interest

and dividends) and (2) another person can claim you as a dependent on their tax return.

Basic Instructions. Employees who are not exempt should complete the Personal Allowances Worksheet. Additional worksheets are provided on page 2 for employees to adjust their withholding allowances based on itemized deductions, adjustments to income, or two-earner/two-job situations. Complete all worksheets that apply to your situation. The worksheets will help you figure the number of withholding allowances you are entitled to claim. However, you may claim fewer allowances than this.

Head of Household. Generally, you may claim head of household filing status on your tax return only if you are unmarried and pay more than 50% of the costs of keeping up a home for yourself and your dependent(s) or other qualifying individuals.

Nonwage Income. If you have a large amount of nonwage income, such as interest or dividends, you should consider making

estimated tax payments using Form 1040-ES. Otherwise, you may find that you owe additional tax at the end of the year.

Two Earners/Two Jobs. If you have a working spouse or more than one job, figure the total number of allowances you are entitled to claim on all jobs using worksheets from only one Form W-4. This total should be divided among all jobs. Your withholding will usually be most accurate when all allowances are claimed on the W-4 filed for the highest paying job and zero allowances are claimed for the others.

Check Your Withholding. After your W-4 takes effect, you can use Pub. 919, Is My Withholding Correct for 1995?, to see how the dollar amount you are having withheld compares to your estimated total annual tax. We recommend you get Pub. 919 especially if you used the Two Earner/Two Job Worksheet and your earnings exceed $150,000 (Single) or $200,000 (Married). Call 1-800-829-3676 to order Pub. 919. Check your telephone directory for the IRS assistance number for further help.

Personal Allowances Worksheet

A Enter "1" for **yourself** if no one else can claim you as a dependent . . . . **A** _____

B Enter "1" if: {
- You are single and have only one job; or
- You are married, have only one job, and your spouse does not work; or
- Your wages from a second job or your spouse's wages (or the total of both) are $1,000 or less.
} . . **B** _____

C Enter "1" for your **spouse.** But, you may choose to enter -0- if you are married and have either a working spouse or more than one job (this may help you avoid having too little tax withheld) . . . . **C** _____

D Enter number of **dependents** (other than your spouse or yourself) you will claim on your tax return . . . . **D** _____

E Enter "1" if you will file as **head of household** on your tax return (see conditions under **Head of Household** above) . **E** _____

F Enter "1" if you have at least $1,500 of **child or dependent care expenses** for which you plan to claim a credit . . **F** _____

G Add lines A through F and enter total here. **Note:** This amount may be different from the number of exemptions you claim on your return ▶ **G** _____

For accuracy, do all worksheets that apply.
- If you plan to **itemize or claim adjustments to income** and want to reduce your withholding, see the Deductions and Adjustments Worksheet on page 2.
- If you are **single** and have **more than one job** and your combined earnings from all jobs exceed $30,000 **OR** if you are **married** and have a **working spouse** or **more than one job,** and the combined earnings from all jobs exceed $50,000, see the Two-Earner/Two-Job Worksheet on page 2 if you want to avoid having too little tax withheld.
- If **neither** of the above situations applies, **stop here** and enter the number from line G on line 5 of Form W-4 below.

-------------------- **Cut here and give the certificate to your employer. Keep the top portion for your records.** --------------------

Form **W-4**
Department of the Treasury
Internal Revenue Service

Employee's Withholding Allowance Certificate

▶ **For Privacy Act and Paperwork Reduction Act Notice, see reverse.**

OMB No. 1545-0010

1995

1 Type or print your first name and middle initial	Last name	2 Your social security number

Home address (number and street or rural route)	3 ☐ Single ☐ Married ☐ Married, but withhold at higher Single rate. **Note:** If married, but legally separated, or spouse is a nonresident alien, check the Single box.

City or town, state, and ZIP code	4 If your last name differs from that on your social security card, check here and call 1-800-772-1213 for a new card . . . . . . ▶ ☐

5 Total number of allowances you are claiming (from line G above or from the worksheets on page 2 if they apply) . **5** _____

6 Additional amount, if any, you want withheld from each paycheck . . . . **6** $ _____

7 I claim exemption from withholding for 1995 and I certify that I meet **BOTH** of the following conditions for exemption:
- Last year I had a right to a refund of **ALL** Federal income tax withheld because I had **NO** tax liability; **AND**
- This year I expect a refund of **ALL** Federal income tax withheld because I expect to have **NO** tax liability.

If you meet both conditions, enter "EXEMPT" here . . . . ▶ **7**

Under penalties of perjury, I certify that I am entitled to the number of withholding allowances claimed on this certificate or entitled to claim exempt status.

Employee's signature ▶ _____ Date ▶ _____ 19 ____

8 Employer's name and address (Employer: Complete 8 and 10 only if sending to the IRS)	9 Office code (optional)	10 Employer identification number

Cat. No. 10220Q

Appendix G: IRS FORM 5305-SEP

Form **5305-SEP**
(Rev. March 1994)
Department of the Treasury
Internal Revenue Service

**Simplified Employee Pension-Individual
Retirement Accounts Contribution Agreement**

(Under Section 408(k) of the Internal Revenue Code)

_____ makes the following agreement under the terms of section 408(k) of the
(Business name – employer)
Internal Revenue Code and the instructions to this form.

Article I—Eligibility Requirements (Check appropriate boxes—see **Specific Instructions.**)

The employer agrees to provide for discretionary contributions in each calendar year to the individual retirement account or individual retirement annuity (IRA) of all employees who are at least _____ years old (not to exceed 21 years old) and have performed services for the employer in at least _____ years (not to exceed 3 years) of the immediately preceding 5 years. This simplified employee pension (SEP) ☐ includes ☐ does not include employees covered under a collective bargaining agreement. ☐ includes ☐ does not include certain nonresident aliens. and ☐ includes ☐ does not include employees whose total compensation during the year is less than $396*.

Article II—SEP Requirements (See **Specific Instructions.**)

The employer agrees that contributions made on behalf of each eligible employee will be:

A. Based only on the first $150,000 of compensation.

B. Made in an amount that is the same percentage of total compensation for every employee.

C. Limited annually to the smaller of $30,000* or 15% of compensation.

D. Paid to the employee's IRA trustee, custodian, or insurance company (for an annuity contract).

Signature Line:

_____ ___/___/___   _____ ___/___/___
Employer's Signature   Date   Employee's Signature   Date

_____
By

143

Form **5305A-SEP**
(Rev. March 1994)
Department of the Treasury
Internal Revenue Service

**Salary Reduction and Other Elective Simplified
Employee Pension-Individual Retirement Accounts
Contribution Agreement
(Under Section 408(k) of the Internal Revenue Code)**

OMB No. 1545-1012
Expires 3-31-96

**DO NOT File with
the Internal
Revenue Service**

_____ establishes the following Model Elective SEP under section 408(k) of the Internal Revenue Code and the instructions to this form.
Name of employer

Article I—Eligibility Requirements (Check appropriate boxes—see instructions.)

Provided the requirements of Article III are met, the employer agrees to permit elective deferrals to be made in each calendar year to the individual retirement accounts or individual retirement annuities

(IRAs), established by or for all employees who are at least _____ years old (not to exceed 21 years) and have performed services for the employer in at least _____ years (not to exceed 3 years) of the immediately preceding 5 years. This simplified employee pension (SEP) ☐ includes ☐ does not include employees covered under a collective bargaining agreement, ☐ includes ☐ does not include certain nonresident aliens, and ☐ includes ☐ does not include employees whose total compensation during the year is less than $396*.

Article II—Elective Deferrals (See instructions.)

A. Salary Reduction Option. An eligible employee may elect to have his or her compensation reduced by the following percentage or amount per pay period, as designated in writing to the employer. Check appropriate box(es) and fill in the blanks.

1. ☐ An amount not in excess of _____% (not to exceed 15%) of an eligible employee's compensation.

2. ☐ An amount not in excess of $_____ .

B. Cash Bonus Option. An eligible employee may base elective deferrals on bonuses that, at the employee's election, may be contributed to the SEP or received in cash during the calendar year. Check if elective deferrals on bonuses may be made to this SEP . . . . ▶ ☐

C. Timing of Elective Deferrals. No deferral election may be based on compensation an eligible employee received, or had a right to receive, before execution of the deferral election.

Article III—SEP Requirements (See instructions.)

The employer agrees that each employee's elective deferrals to the SEP will be:

A. Based only on the first $150,000 of compensation.

B. Limited annually to the smaller of: **(1)** 15% of compensation; **or (2)** $9,240*.

C. Limited further, under section 415, if the employer also maintains another SEP.

D. Paid to the employee's IRA trustee, custodian, or insurance company (for an annuity contract) or, if necessary, an IRA established for an employee by the employer.

E. Made only if at least 50% of the employer's employees eligible to participate elect to have amounts contributed to the SEP. If the 50% requirement is not satisfied as of the end of any calendar year, then all of the elective deferrals made by the employees for that calendar year will be considered "disallowed deferrals," i.e., IRA contributions that are not SEP-IRA contributions.

F. Made only if the employer had 25 or fewer employees eligible to participate at all times during the prior calendar year.

G. Adjusted only if deferrals to this SEP for any calendar year do not meet the "deferral percentage limitation" described in SECTION IV.

Article IV—Excess SEP Contributions (See instructions.)

Elective deferrals by a "highly compensated employee" must satisfy the deferral percentage limitation under section 408(k)(6)(A)(iii). Amounts in excess of this limitation will be deemed excess SEP contributions for the affected highly compensated employee or employees.

Article V—Notice Requirements (See instructions.)

A. The employer will notify each highly compensated employee, by March 15 following the end of the calendar year to which any excess SEP contributions relate, of the excess SEP contributions to the highly compensated employee's SEP-IRA for the applicable year. The notification will specify the amount of the excess SEP, the calendar year in which the contributions are includible in income, and must provide an explanation of applicable penalties if the excess contributions are not withdrawn on time.

B. The employer will notify each employee who makes an elective deferral to a SEP that, until March 15 after the year of the deferral, any transfer or distribution from that employee's SEP-IRA of SEP contributions (or income on these contributions) attributable to elective deferrals made that year will be includible in income for purposes of sections 72(t) and 408(d)(1).

C. The employer will notify each employee by March 15 of each year of any disallowed deferrals to the employee's SEP-IRA for the preceding calendar year. Such notification will specify the amount of the disallowed deferrals and the calendar year in which those deferrals are includible in income and must provide an explanation of applicable penalties if the disallowed deferrals are not withdrawn on time.

Article VI—Top-Heavy Requirements (See instructions.)

A. Unless paragraph B below is checked, the employer will satisfy the top-heavy requirements of section 416 by making a minimum contribution each year to the SEP-IRA of each employee eligible to participate in this SEP (other than a key employee defined in section 416(i)). This contribution, in combination with other nonelective contributions, if any, is equal to the smaller of 3% of each eligible nonkey employee's compensation or a percentage of such compensation equal to the percentage of compensation at which elective and nonelective contributions are made under this SEP (and any other SEP maintained by the employer) for the year for the key employee for whom such percentage is the highest for the year.

B. ☐ The top-heavy requirements of section 416 will be satisfied through contributions to nonkey employees' SEP-IRAs under this employer's nonelective SEP.

C. To satisfy the minimum contribution requirement under section 416, all nonelective SEP contributions will be taken into account but elective deferrals will not be taken into account.

Article VII—Effective Date (See instructions.)

This SEP will be effective upon adoption and establishment of IRAs for all eligible employees.

Changes to Elective SEP Deferrals

1. A participant may elect to begin Elective SEP Deferrals as of _____ / _____ / _____ . [ENTER AT LEAST ONE DATE DURING A CALENDAR YEAR.] Such election shall become effective as of the pay period following the election or as soon as administratively feasible thereafter. A participant's election to have Elective Deferrals made pursuant to a salary reduction agreement shall remain in effect until modified or terminated.

2. An election to change or terminate the Elective SEP Deferral percentage or amounts can be made on _____ / _____ / _____ . [ENTER AT LEAST ONE DATE DURING A CALENDAR YEAR.] Such change will become effective as of the pay period following the election or as soon as administratively feasible thereafter.

IRA Adoption Information My Individual Retirement Account has been established with:

Custodian or Trustee _____

Address _____

IRA Account Number _____

City, State, ZIP _____

Signature Line:

_____ _____ / _____ / _____
Employer's Signature   Date

_____ _____ / _____ / _____
Employee's Signature   Date

By _____

144

Appendix H: IRS FORM 1040 SCHEDULE C

SCHEDULE C
(Form 1040)

Department of the Treasury
Internal Revenue Service (R)

Profit or Loss From Business
(Sole Proprietorship)

▶ Partnerships, joint ventures, etc., must file Form 1065.

▶ Attach to Form 1040 or Form 1041. ▶ See Instructions for Schedule C (Form 1040).

OMB No. 1545-0074

1994

Attachment
Sequence No. 09

Name of proprietor | Social security number (SSN)

A Principal business or profession, including product or service (see page C-1) | **B** Enter principal business code (see page C-6) ▶

C Business name. if no separate business name. leave blank. | **D** Employer ID number (EIN), if any

E Business address (including suite or room no.) ▶ ....
City, town or post office, state, and ZIP code

F Accounting method: (1) ☐ Cash (2) ☐ Accrual (3) ☐ Other (specify) ▶ ....

G Method(s) used to value closing inventory: (1) ☐ Cost (2) ☐ Lower of cost or market (3) ☐ Other (attach explanation) (4) ☐ Does not apply (if checked, skip line H) | Yes | No

H Was there any change in determining quantities, costs, or valuations between opening and closing inventory? If "Yes," attach explanation

I Did you "materially participate" in the operation of this business during 1994? If "No," see page C-2 for limit on losses.

J If you started or acquired this business during 1994. check here ▶ ☐

Part I Income

1 Gross receipts or sales. **Caution:** If this income was reported to you on Form W-2 and the "Statutory employee" box on that form was checked, see page C-2 and check here ▶ ☐ | 1 |
2 Returns and allowances | 2 |
3 Subtract line 2 from line 1 | 3 |
4 Cost of goods sold (from line 40 on page 2) | 4 |
5 **Gross profit.** Subtract line 4 from line 3 | 5 |
6 Other income, including Federal and state gasoline or fuel tax credit or refund (see page C-2) | 6 |
7 **Gross income.** Add lines 5 and 6 ▶ | 7 |

Part II Expenses. Enter expenses for business use of your home **only** on line 30.

8 Advertising	8		19 Pension and profit-sharing plans	19	
9 Bad debts from sales or services (see page C-3)	9		20 Rent or lease (see page C-4):		
			a Vehicles, machinery, and equipment	20a	
10 Car and truck expenses (see page C-3)	10		b Other business property	20b	
11 Commissions and fees	11		21 Repairs and maintenance	21	
12 Depletion	12		22 Supplies (not included in Part III)	22	
13 Depreciation and section 179 expense deduction (not included in Part III) (see page C-3)	13		23 Taxes and licenses	23	
			24 Travel, meals, and entertainment:		
14 Employee benefit programs (other than on line 19)	14		a Travel	24a	
15 Insurance (other than health)	15		b Meals and entertainment		
16 Interest:			c Enter 50% of line 24b subject to limitations (see page C-4)		
a Mortgage (paid to banks, etc.)	16a		d Subtract line 24c from line 24b	24d	
b Other	16b		25 Utilities	25	
17 Legal and professional services	17		26 Wages (less employment credits)	26	
18 Office expense	18		27 Other expenses (from line 46 on page 2)	27	

28 **Total expenses** before expenses for business use of home. Add lines 8 through 27 in columns. ▶ | 28 |
29 Tentative profit (loss). Subtract line 28 from line 7 | 29 |
30 Expenses for business use of your home. Attach **Form 8829** | 30 |
31 **Net profit or (loss).** Subtract line 30 from line 29.

  • If a profit, enter on **Form 1040, line 12,** and ALSO on **Schedule SE, line 2** (statutory employees. see page C-5). Estates and trusts. enter on Form 1041, line 3. | 31 |

  • If a loss, you MUST go on to line 32.

32 If you have a loss. check the box that describes your investment in this activity (see page C-5).

  • If you checked 32a. enter the loss on **Form 1040, line 12,** and ALSO on **Schedule SE, line 2** (statutory employees. see page C-5). Estates and trusts. enter on Form 1041, line 3. | 32a ☐ All investment is at risk.
  | 32b ☐ Some investment is not at risk.

  • If you checked 32b. you MUST attach **Form 6198.**

For **Paperwork Reduction Act Notice, see Form 1040 instructions.**   Cat. No. 11334P   Schedule C (Form 1040) 1994

Part III   **Cost of Goods Sold** (see page C-5)

33	Inventory at beginning of year. If different from last year's closing inventory, attach explanation . .	33	
34	Purchases less cost of items withdrawn for personal use	34	
35	Cost of labor. Do not include salary paid to yourself	35	
36	Materials and supplies	36	
37	Other costs	37	
38	Add lines 33 through 37	38	
39	Inventory at end of year	39	
40	**Cost of goods sold.** Subtract line 39 from line 38. Enter the result here and on page 1, line 4 . .	40	

Part IV   **Information on Your Vehicle.** Complete this part **ONLY** if you are claiming car or truck expenses on line 10 and are not required to file Form 4562 for this business. See the instructions for line 13 on page C-3 to find out if you must file.

41   When did you place your vehicle in service for business purposes? (month, day, year) ▶ ..../............/............ .

42   Of the total number of miles you drove your vehicle during 1994, enter the number of miles you used your vehicle for:

a   Business .... b Commuting .... c Other ....

43   Do you (or your spouse) have another vehicle available for personal use? . . . . ☐ Yes   ☐ No

44   Was your vehicle available for use during off-duty hours? . . . . ☐ Yes   ☐ No

45a   Do you have evidence to support your deduction? . . . . ☐ Yes   ☐ No
   b   If "Yes," is the evidence written? . . . . ☐ Yes   ☐ No

Part V   **Other Expenses.** List below business expenses not included on lines 8–26 or line 30.

....		
....		
....		
....		
....		
....		
....		
....		
....		
....		

46	**Total other expenses.** Enter here and on page 1, line 27	46	

Appendix I: IRS FORM 1065

Form **1065**	**U.S. Partnership Return of Income**	OMB No. 1545-0099
Department of the Treasury Internal Revenue Service	For calendar year 1994, or tax year beginning .... , 1994, and ending .... , 19 .... . ▶ **See separate instructions.**	**1994**

A Principal business activity	Use the IRS label. Other- wise, please print or type.	Name of partnership	D Employer identification number
B Principal product or service		Number, street, and room or suite no. (If a P.O. box, see page 9 of the instructions.)	E Date business started
C Business code number		City or town, state, and ZIP code	F Total assets (see Specific Instructions) $

G Check applicable boxes: **(1)** ☐ Initial return   **(2)** ☐ Final return   **(3)** ☐ Change in address   **(4)** ☐ Amended return
H Check accounting method: **(1)** ☐ Cash   **(2)** ☐ Accrual   **(3)** ☐ Other (specify) ▶ ....
I Number of Schedules K-1. Attach one for each person who was a partner at any time during the tax year ▶ ....

Caution: *Include only trade or business income and expenses on lines 1a through 22 below. See the instructions for more information.*

Income

1a	Gross receipts or sales	1a	
b	Less returns and allowances	1b	
			1c
2	Cost of goods sold (Schedule A, line 8)		2
3	Gross profit. Subtract line 2 from line 1c		3
4	Ordinary income (loss) from other partnerships, estates, and trusts (attach schedule) .		4
5	Net farm profit (loss) (attach Schedule F (Form 1040))		5
6	Net gain (loss) from Form 4797, Part II, line 20.		6
7	Other income (loss) (see instructions) (attach schedule)		7
8	**Total income (loss).** Combine lines 3 through 7		8

Deductions (see instructions for limitations)

9	Salaries and wages (other than to partners) (less employment credits) .		9
10	Guaranteed payments to partners		10
11	Repairs and maintenance		11
12	Bad debts		12
13	Rent		13
14	Taxes and licenses		14
15	Interest		15
16a	Depreciation (see instructions)	16a	
b	Less depreciation reported on Schedule A and elsewhere on return	16b	16c
17	Depletion (**Do not deduct oil and gas depletion.**)		17
18	Retirement plans, etc.		18
19	Employee benefit programs		19
20	Other deductions (attach schedule)		20
21	**Total deductions.** Add the amounts shown in the far right column for lines 9 through 20 .		21
22	**Ordinary income (loss)** from trade or business activities. Subtract line 21 from line 8 . .		22

Please Sign Here	Under penalties of perjury, I declare that I have examined this return, including accompanying schedules and statements, and to the best of my knowledge and belief, it is true, correct, and complete. Declaration of preparer (other than general partner) is based on all information of which preparer has any knowledge.		
	▶ Signature of general partner or limited liability company member		▶ Date

Paid Preparer's Use Only	Preparer's signature ▶	Date	Check if self-employed ▶ ☐	Preparer's social security no.
	Firm's name (or yours if self-employed) and address ▶		E.I. No. ▶	
			ZIP code ▶	

For Paperwork Reduction Act Notice, see page 1 of separate instructions.   Cat. No. 11390Z   Form **1065** (1994)

Schedule A   Cost of Goods Sold

1 Inventory at beginning of year	**1**	
2 Purchases less cost of items withdrawn for personal use	**2**	
3 Cost of labor.	**3**	
4 Additional section 263A costs (see instructions) *(attach schedule)*	**4**	
5 Other costs *(attach schedule)*	**5**	
6 **Total.** Add lines 1 through 5	**6**	
7 Inventory at end of year	**7**	
8 **Cost of goods sold.** Subtract line 7 from line 6. Enter here and on page 1, line 2	**8**	

9a Check all methods used for valuing closing inventory:

    (i) ☐ Cost

    (ii) ☐ Lower of cost or market as described in Regulations section 1.471-4

    (iii) ☐ Writedown of "subnormal" goods as described in Regulations section 1.471-2(c)

    (iv) ☐ Other (specify method used and attach explanation) ▶ ....

  b Check this box if the LIFO inventory method was adopted this tax year for any goods *(if checked, attach Form 970)* . . ▶ ☐

  c Do the rules of section 263A (for property produced or acquired for resale) apply to the partnership? . . . ☐ **Yes** ☐ **No**

  d Was there any change in determining quantities, cost, or valuations between opening and closing inventory? ☐ **Yes** ☐ **No**
    If "Yes," attach explanation.

Schedule B   Other Information

	Yes	No
1 What type of entity is filing this return? Check the applicable box ▶ ☐ General partnership ☐ Limited partnership ☐ Limited liability company		
2 Are any partners in this partnership also partnerships?.		
3 Is this partnership a partner in another partnership?		
4 Is this partnership subject to the consolidated audit procedures of sections 6221 through 6233? If "Yes," see **Designation of Tax Matters Partner** below		
5 Does this partnership meet **ALL THREE** of the following requirements?		
a The partnership's total receipts for the tax year were less than $250,000;		
b The partnership's total assets at the end of the tax year were less than $600,000; **AND**		
c Schedules K-1 are filed with the return and furnished to the partners on or before the due date (including extensions) for the partnership return.		
If "Yes," the partnership is not required to complete Schedules L, M-1, and M-2; Item F on page 1 of Form 1065; or Item J on Schedule K-1		
6 Does this partnership have any foreign partners?		
7 Is this partnership a publicly traded partnership as defined in section 469(k)(2)?		
8 Has this partnership filed, or is it required to file, **Form 8264,** Application for Registration of a Tax Shelter? . .		
9 At any time during calendar year 1994, did the partnership have an interest in or a signature or other authority over a financial account in a foreign country (such as a bank account, securities account, or other financial account)? (See the instructions for exceptions and filing requirements for Form TD F 90-22.1.) If "Yes," enter the name of the foreign country. ▶		
10 Was the partnership the grantor of, or transferor to, a foreign trust that existed during the current tax year, whether or not the partnership or any partner has any beneficial interest in it? If "Yes," you may have to file Forms 3520, 3520-A, or 926		
11 Was there a distribution of property or a transfer (e.g., by sale or death) of a partnership interest during the tax year? If "Yes," you may elect to adjust the basis of the partnership's assets under section 754 by attaching the statement described under **Elections Made By the Partnership**		

Designation of Tax Matters Partner (See instructions.)

Enter below the general partner designated as the tax matters partner (TMP) for the tax year of this return:

Name of designated TMP ▶		Identifying number of TMP ▶	
Address of designated TMP ▶			

Appendix J: IRS FORM 1120S

Form **1120S** Department of the Treasury Internal Revenue Service	**U.S. Income Tax Return for an S Corporation** ▶ Do not file this form unless the corporation has timely filed Form 2553 to elect to be an S corporation. ▶ See separate instructions.	OMB No. 1545-0130 **1994**

For calendar year 1994, or tax year beginning _____ 1994, and ending _____ , 19___

A Date of election as an S corporation	**Use IRS label. Other- wise, please print or type.**	Name	C Employer identification number
		Number, street, and room or suite no. (If a P.O. box, see page 9 of the instructions.)	D Date incorporated
B Business code no. (see Specific Instructions)		City or town, state, and ZIP code	E Total assets (see Specific Instructions) $

F Check applicable boxes: (1) ☐ Initial return   (2) ☐ Final return   (3) ☐ Change in address   (4) ☐ Amended return
G Check this box if this S corporation is subject to the consolidated audit procedures of sections 6241 through 6245 (see instructions before checking this box) . ▶ ☐
H Enter number of shareholders in the corporation at end of the tax year . . . . ▶

Caution: *Include only trade or business income and expenses on lines 1a through 21. See the instructions for more information.*

Income

1a	Gross receipts or sales _____	b Less returns and allowances _____	c Bal ▶	1c	
2	Cost of goods sold (Schedule A, line 8)	2	
3	Gross profit. Subtract line 2 from line 1c	3	
4	Net gain (loss) from Form 4797, Part II, line 20 *(attach Form 4797)* . . .	4	
5	Other income (loss) (see instructions) *(attach schedule)*	5	
6	**Total income (loss).** Combine lines 3 through 5 . . . . ▶	6	

Deductions (See instructions for limitations.)

7	Compensation of officers	7	
8	Salaries and wages (less employment credits)	8	
9	Repairs and maintenance	9	
10	Bad debts	10	
11	Rents	11	
12	Taxes and licenses	12	
13	Interest	13	
14a	Depreciation (see instructions)	14a	
b	Depreciation claimed on Schedule A and elsewhere on return . .	14b	
c	Subtract line 14b from line 14a	14c	
15	Depletion **(Do not deduct oil and gas depletion.)**	15	
16	Advertising	16	
17	Pension, profit-sharing, etc., plans	17	
18	Employee benefit programs	18	
19	Other deductions (see instructions) *(attach schedule)*	19	
20	**Total deductions.** Add the amounts shown in the far right column for lines 7 through 19 . ▶	20	
21	Ordinary income (loss) from trade or business activities. Subtract line 20 from line 6	21	

Tax and Payments

22	Tax: a Excess net passive income tax *(attach schedule)* . . .	22a	
	b Tax from Schedule D (Form 1120S)	22b	
	c Add lines 22a and 22b (see instructions for additional taxes) . . .	22c	
23	Payments: a 1994 estimated tax payments and amount applied from 1993 return	23a	
	b Tax deposited with Form 7004	23b	
	c Credit for Federal tax paid on fuels *(attach Form 4136)*	23c	
	d Add lines 23a through 23c	23d	
24	Estimated tax penalty (see instructions). Check if Form 2220 is attached . . . . ▶ ☐	24	
25	**Tax due.** If the total of lines 22c and 24 is larger than line 23d, enter amount owed. See instructions for depositary method of payment	25	
26	**Overpayment.** If line 23d is larger than the total of lines 22c and 24, enter amount overpaid ▶	26	
27	Enter amount of line 26 you want: **Credited to 1995 estimated tax** ▶ _____	Refunded ▶	27	

Please Sign Here	Under penalties of perjury, I declare that I have examined this return, including accompanying schedules and statements, and to the best of my knowledge and belief, it is true, correct, and complete. Declaration of preparer (other than taxpayer) is based on all information of which preparer has any knowledge.
	▶ _____ Signature of officer Date _____ Title _____

Paid Preparer's Use Only	Preparer's signature ▶ _____	Date _____	Check if self-employed ▶ ☐	Preparer's social security number _____
	Firm's name (or yours if self-employed) and address ▶ _____		E.I. No. ▶ _____ ZIP code ▶ _____	

For Paperwork Reduction Act Notice, see page 1 of separate instructions.   Cat. No. 11510H   Form **1120S** (1994)

149

Schedule A   Cost of Goods Sold (See instructions.)

1	Inventory at beginning of year	1	
2	Purchases	2	
3	Cost of labor	3	
4	Additional section 263A costs (see instructions) (attach schedule)	4	
5	Other costs (attach schedule)	5	
6	**Total.** Add lines 1 through 5	6	
7	Inventory at end of year	7	
8	**Cost of goods sold.** Subtract line 7 from line 6. Enter here and on page 1, line 2	8	

9a Check all methods used for valuing closing inventory:

   (i) ☐ Cost

   (ii) ☐ Lower of cost or market as described in Regulations section 1.471-4

   (iii) ☐ Writedown of "subnormal" goods as described in Regulations section 1.471-2(c)

   (iv) ☐ Other (specify method used and attach explanation) ▶ ....

  b Check if the LIFO inventory method was adopted this tax year for any goods (if checked, attach Form 970). . . . . . ▶ ☐

  c If the LIFO inventory method was used for this tax year, enter percentage (or amounts) of closing

    inventory computed under LIFO **9c**

  d Do the rules of section 263A (for property produced or acquired for resale) apply to the corporation? . . . . ☐ Yes ☐ No

  e Was there any change in determining quantities, cost, or valuations between opening and closing inventory? . . ☐ Yes ☐ No
    If "Yes," attach explanation.

Schedule B   Other Information

		Yes	No
1	Check method of accounting: (a) ☐ Cash (b) ☐ Accrual (c) ☐ Other (specify) ▶		
2	Refer to the list in the instructions and state the corporation's principal:		
	(a) Business activity ▶ .... (b) Product or service ▶		
3	Did the corporation at the end of the tax year own, directly or indirectly, 50% or more of the voting stock of a domestic corporation? (For rules of attribution, see section 267(c).) If "Yes," attach a schedule showing: (a) name, address, and employer identification number and (b) percentage owned.		
4	Was the corporation a member of a controlled group subject to the provisions of section 1561?		
5	At any time during calendar year 1994, did the corporation have an interest in or a signature or other authority over a financial account in a foreign country (such as a bank account, securities account, or other financial account)? (See instructions for exceptions and filing requirements for Form TD F 90-22.1.)		
	If "Yes," enter the name of the foreign country ▶		
6	Was the corporation the grantor of, or transferor to, a foreign trust that existed during the current tax year, whether or not the corporation has any beneficial interest in it? If "Yes," the corporation may have to file Forms 3520, 3520-A, or 926		
7	Check this box if the corporation has filed or is required to file **Form 8264,** Application for Registration of a Tax Shelter . . . . ▶ ☐		
8	Check this box if the corporation issued publicly offered debt instruments with original issue discount . . ▶ ☐		
	If so, the corporation may have to file **Form 8281,** Information Return for Publicly Offered Original Issue Discount Instruments.		
9	If the corporation: (a) filed its election to be an S corporation after 1986, (b) was a C corporation before it elected to be an S corporation or the corporation acquired an asset with a basis determined by reference to its basis (or the basis of any other property) in the hands of a C corporation, and (c) has net unrealized built-in gain (defined in section 1374(d)(1)) in excess of the net recognized built-in gain from prior years, enter the net unrealized built-in gain reduced by net recognized built-in gain from prior years (see instructions) . . . . . . ▶ $		
10	Check this box if the corporation had subchapter C earnings and profits at the close of the tax year (see instructions) . . . . ▶ ☐		

Designation of Tax Matters Person (See instructions.)

Enter below the shareholder designated as the tax matters person (TMP) for the tax year of this return:

Name of
designated TMP ▶ _____

Identifying
number of TMP ▶ _____

Address of
designated TMP ▶ _____

INDEX

ABOUT THE AUTHOR

HENRY AIY'M FELLMAN has served small businesses as an attorney, accountant, and financial adviser for over twenty years. His expertise is taxation, especially as it relates to the self employed.

Henry Aiy'm Fellman attended undergraduate school at the University of Bridgeport, where he majored in Accounting. After graduating in 1972, he entered Brooklyn Law School, where he received his Juris Doctor in 1975. He is licensed to practice law in Colorado, New Mexico, Arizona and New York. From 1975 till 1978, after working in the tax law department of one of the Big 8 CPA firms, he started his own private practice, which he has had for the past 17 years.

In 1987, he co-founded the Business Success Institute in Boulder, Colorado, where he created and taught workshops to owners of small businesses in subjects related to tax planning, accounting, finances, and start-ups. He has also taught and lectured at the University of Colorado, Rutgers University, Boulder Graduate College, the Economic Institute, Boulder Chamber of Commerce, Win/Win, Rocky Mountain Inventors Congress, and Barnes Business School.

He co-hosted a radio talk show and has written numerous articles and publications on taxes and business-related topics.

Know someone who'd like a copy of this book? To order additional copies please mail this form, or call 24 hours a day.

☐ Please send me _____ copies of *"How to Keep Your Hard-Earned Money"* at just $17.95 each, plus $3.90 shipping and handling per order.
☐ I don't need another copy today, but please keep me informed of future updates.

Name_____Business_____

Address _____

City, State, Zip _____Telephone ( )_____
☐ My check is enclosed for $_____ (Make check payable to Solutions Press)
☐ Charge to my credit card: ☐ MasterCard   ☐ Visa

Cardholder's name _____Signature _____

Card number _____Exp. date _____

Mail to: Solutions Press, Inc.   Or call anytime:
2888 Bluff St., Suite 256
Boulder, Colorado 80301   1-800-211-0544

- -

Know someone who'd like a copy of this book? To order additional copies please mail this form, or call 24 hours a day.

☐ Please send me _____ copies of *"How to Keep Your Hard-Earned Money"* at just $17.95 each, plus $3.90 shipping and handling per order.
☐ I don't need another copy today, but please keep me informed of future updates.

Name_____Business_____

Address _____

City, State, Zip _____Telephone ( )_____
☐ My check is enclosed for $_____ (Make check payable to Solutions Press)
☐ Charge to my credit card: ☐ Mastercard   ☐ Visa

Cardholders name _____Signature _____

Card number _____Exp. date _____

Mail to: Solutions Press, Inc.   Or call anytime:
2888 Bluff St., Suite 256
Boulder, Colorado 80301   1-800-211-0544

- -

Henry Fellman is available for seminars and private consulting. If you or your association or professional group would be interested in hosting a *"Keep What You Earn"* Workshop or on learning more about how to apply the ideas in this book, please contact him at 303-782-6571.